Excuse Me Sir…
Do You Speak Dog

By Bryan Litchford CPDT-KA

ISBN# 978-0-578-46997-3

Contents

Introduction

For the past twenty years I have made a living as a guitar teacher. In that time I've come to realize that there are basically three kinds of student. There is the passionate student that absolutely loves playing the guitar and devotes all of their available time to learning the craft almost to the point of obsession. Then you have the casual learner who enjoys playing and is willing to put in enough practice time to at least learn the basics. I like to call them the campfire guitarist. Lastly, you have the poser. These students love the idea of playing guitar but never even look at their guitar between lessons. They are not willing to put in the work required, and so their guitar is destined to end up in the closet never to be seen again, or sold to a pawn shop in order to pursue their next endeavor.

So why is a dog trainer talking about guitars? Well, as a trainer, and as a training and behavior consultant volunteer at a local dog shelter, I have noticed a similarity in the way people approach dog ownership. You have those who devote everything they have to caring for dogs. They are not only totally devoted to their personal dogs, but will also do anything and everything they can to help other dogs that are not so fortunate. Then you have the casual dog owner who enjoys dogs and does what is required to keep their dog happy and healthy including healthy food, a warm place to sleep, training, mental stimulation, and enrichment. Unfortunately, the next group also exists, and is part of the reason I am writing this book.

This group loves the idea of having a dog but are not willing to put in the time and resources needed to keep their dog physically and mentally healthy. I like to think that it's due to a lack of understanding of what is required, much like the guitar student I spoke of before. The dogs in their care are the ones that usually end up at the shelter, or worse, dumped on the side of the road. The vast majority of the time, behavioral issues are cited as the reason they gave up on their pet. Writing this book is my attempt at educating the public as to the importance of training their dogs to coexist in our homes without conflict, and by doing so, result in the reduction of this last group. After all a discarded guitar, although bothersome to me, is just an object. No one is hurt if it gets stowed away in the attic or ends up in the landfill, but dogs are not objects. They are living, breathing creatures that we humans have taken upon ourselves to shape into beings dependant on us for survival.

It's my hope that my love for dogs, and love of teaching people, will be reflected in this book, and the wisdom I offer will not fall on blind eyes, so the relationship between humans and dogs will be in some small way repaired and cultivated.

So how do I help struggling dogs stay in their homes? What is one thing that would make a tremendous impact on people and their relationship with their dogs?

Communication! That's it! I have yet to be hired by anyone for dog training that does not struggle with how to communicate with their dog, and why wouldn't they? We are two very different species. We don't speak the same language, and we don't have the same needs and wants. Imagine you're in a foreign country that you have never been to before.

It is a very different culture with a different language, and the people there have very different customs from your own. Many of the day to day practices that are normal where you come from are considered offensive to them. How difficult would it be to fit in? How would you perform even the most basic tasks like calling a cab or ordering food at a restaurant? Without a guide or someone who could interpret for you, it would feel impossible. You might even get yourself into a bit of trouble if not careful.

We ask our dogs to live in that kind of scenario every day. We expect them to behave like humans, to understand everything we say, to do everything we ask; and when they try to show us what they need, we ignore them or punish them for what appears to us as bad behavior.

Obviously, dogs have a limited ability to learn our language, but if taught in a more visual way that makes sense to the dog, you would be surprised just how many words a dog can learn. After all even humans need to be shown.

I recall an incident when my son was young. I was doing repairs on my old junker car that wouldn't start, and I asked him to hand me a Phillips screwdriver. It was hot, and I was laying on the ground in a puddle of oil, angry that my car broke down at the most inconvenient time possible. I waited for what felt like an eternity, getting more frustrated by the second. I could hear him rustling around in my toolbox where I had several of them. Finally, I exploded with, "what's the holdup?" His reply was, "I don't see anything with Phillip written on it." It was then I realized that although I had shown him what a screwdriver was, I had never shown him what a Phillips head screwdriver looked like.

How many times have you told your dogs to sit or lay down, and they just stare at you? Have you taught them how to sit or lay down?

Maybe previously you told him to sit, and he just happened to be tired of standing and sat. Was there any real communication, or did you just get lucky that his needs and your needs happened to be aligned at that moment? Then there's the flip side of the coin. Are we in tune with the signals our dogs are giving us? Even people who work with dogs every day, including myself, get them wrong, or just simply don't pay attention to them. There are a whole host of clues our dogs give us. Some subtle like yawning, tongue flicking, posture, ear position, blinking and tail position. Then some that are not so subtle like growling, barking, and chewing up your shoes, just to name a few. This last group usually gets our attention, but not in a way that is helpful.

So to sum it up, my goal with this book is to show you how to train your dog specific behaviors, but more importantly, I hope to explain the purpose of training those behaviors, and how you can use them, along with what your dog is showing you, to build better two-way communication with your dog. In my opinion, this is the key to building a strong bond with your dog resulting in an amazing relationship that rivals that of family, and family is not easily discarded.

CHAPTER 1

The Tools For Change

When training your dog, the first step is to know what affects behavior and how to use this information.

Classical Conditioning

Classical conditioning, also known as Pavlovian conditioning (named after the scientist who discovered the phenomenon), occurs when an unconditioned stimulus (a bell) is paired with a conditioned stimulus (food), resulting in a conditioned response (drooling). In plain English: if you ring a bell prior to feeding your dog enough times, your dog will begin drooling, or get excited, any time he hears a bell. This is a physiological response based in emotion, not a decision made by the dog. When training, there is classical conditioning occurring all the time whether we are aware of it or not. Anytime we play with our dog, feed our dog, or just give them access to something they want, there is potentially classical conditioning occurring. It is our most powerful tool in effecting change.

Operant Conditioning

Through operant conditioning an individual makes an association between a particular behavior and a consequence. (B.F. Skinner 1938). In operant conditioning, there are four quadrants, but before exploring these quadrants, it is important to understand what the terms positive and negative mean in this context. Rather than thinking in terms of a positive or negative experience, the term positive = adding something, and the term negative = removing something.

The Four Quadrants
of Operant Conditioning

1. Positive reinforcement - You ask your
   dog to sit. When he complies, he gets
   a treat. Your dog realizes that sitting
   resulted in a treat, so getting your dog
   to sit the next time is easier. Sitting
   has been positively reinforced.

2. Positive punishment - Your dog barks at the neighbors dog. To make him stop, you shock him using a shock collar. Your dog realizes that barking results in an unpleasant shock, so he doesn't bark. Barking has been positively punished.

3. Negative reinforcement - You ask your dog to sit followed by pulling up on his choke collar, cutting off his air supply, and pushing down on his bottom. Your dog sits, and you relieve the pressure. Your dog realizes that sitting resulted in the pressure being removed, so next time he hears the cue to sit, he does so to avoid the pressure. Sitting has been negatively reinforced.

4. Negative punishment - Your dog jumps up on you to get your attention. To make him stop, you turn your back on him and walk away. Your dog realizes that jumping up results in you going away, so your dog stops jumping up. Jumping up has been negatively punished.

Through operant conditioning, we teach our dogs to do specific behaviors, or stop certain behaviors, by pairing those behaviors with a particular outcome. (Example: sit = reward). Although all four of the quadrants can effect change, there are significant, and sometimes dangerous, drawbacks to using aversives like pain or intimidation in training.

We choose LIMA

Personally I consider my dogs to be part of my family and would never want to use any method in training that would cause any kind of pain, physically or emotionally, to my dog. Therefore, when training my pets, or yours, I always adhere to the standards set by LIMA (Least Intrusive Minimally Aversive). So in practical terms: we reward good behavior, hopefully resulting in "positive reinforcement," and an increase of that behavior; and when necessary, we take something they want away for unwanted behavior in hopes of reducing that behavior using "negative punishment."

Positive Reinforcement

Positive reinforcement can be anything that the dog is willing to work for; however, there are certain reinforcers that are built in. These are called primary reinforcers, meaning they are innate. Some examples of primary reinforcers are food, water, air, rest, sex, control of their environment, and behaviors connected to prey drive like sniffing, hunting, chasing, and dissection. Then there are reinforcers like affection, petting, play, and attention. These things can become very reinforcing, but some may need fostering to build the same emotional connection. When training your dog, it is crucial for you to find the reinforcers that your dog is willing to work for at any given time. Example: Humans appreciate a nice thank you, but if you went to work one day and your boss decided to pay you with a heartfelt thank you, you would probably not work there long. A nice loving thank you, or "good dog," may work for reinforcing a sit at home with no distractions, but a stay or a sit at the dog park may require something a bit more substantial, especially if you want him to be a happy, willing participant.

Timing Your Reinforcement

When training your dog, it is important that you show the dog they are on the right track. If you are late giving the reinforcer, it is likely that it won't be paired with the behavior, so no learning has occurred. For a reward to be paired, it needs to be given within one second of the behavior. For this reason, the use of clickers (a noise making device), or use of a marker word like "yes," is a very effective tool. By classically conditioning the clicker, or marker word, to predict that reinforcement is on the way, your accuracy can be substantially improved. More on clickers or marker words, and how to condition them, later.

A perfect example of a reinforcer failing to work is rewarding the dog for pottying outside after he has come back in the house. For the dog to make the connection between relieving himself, and you giving him the cookie, you have to go outside and give the reward at the moment of completion.

Reinforcement Schedules

When I was a child, my parent worked in a factory sewing shirts. The people she worked for needed their workers to get the shirts out as quickly as possible, so on top of their hourly wage, they were given an incentive to work as quickly as possible. For each shirt they completed, they were given a button that represented a few cents which would be added to their pay. This sped up productivity, because the reinforcement came with every shirt they completed.

Continuous Reinforcement Schedule

In training, it is important to show the dog what they are doing is correct. So when teaching something new, pay them each and every time they get it right. This is called a continuous reinforcement schedule. By doing this you are creating excitement about learning the new behavior, and a history of reinforcement, causing them to want to continue.

Variable Reinforcement Schedule

Eventually, you want to vary the reinforcement schedule by randomly choosing behaviors to reinforce and behaviors not to reinforce. Once your dog is excited about the prospect of reward, only reinforce better than average efforts at the behavior. Example: straighter sits, faster downs. This is called a differential reinforcement schedule, and it works to make the dog begin to gamble as to when reinforcement is coming, causing them to try harder to get the reward. This happens every day with humans in casinos all over the country, and it works to make the behavior very durable. To help your dog along, and keep the experience a fun one, cheer your dog on during the reps you are not reinforcing with your primary reinforcers. Example: GOOD DOG! GREAT JOB! THAT A BOY! This is

also how you "fade out treats." However, I would suggest that you should never fade out treats entirely.

The number one rule to remember when training is that **consequence drives behavior**. In other words, if you stopped getting paid, why would you go to work? The answer is you wouldn't, and neither will your dog, unless you force them, and that is not what positive training is about. You have to feed your dog anyway, so why not take advantage of this by teaching them with their food, and maintain a healthy relationship with your best friend rather than one of slave and master.

CHAPTER 2

Training and Management

Setting up for success

One of the reasons it's commonly thought that you can't teach an old dog new tricks is because older dogs have developed habits that humans consider "bad behavior." Breaking those habits can be a challenge, especially if we have unwittingly reinforced those "bad"habits." Puppies, on the other hand, can seem like blank slates just waiting to be written on, but given too much freedom, they will make bad decisions, and it won't be long before you are in the same boat as with an untrained adult dog.

To get started on the right foot, whether it be with a puppy or an adult dog you have recently adopted, you want to control their environment. With a puppy, so that they never have a chance to develop bad habits, and with adult dogs, so that they no longer are able to practice those habits.

Behaviors that are reinforced continue and behaviors that are not reinforced fade. So if your pup is chewing on a table leg, most likely it is because he is teething and it feels good. Since this behavior is self reinforcing to the pup, it will continue, but if he's not given access to it (by being in a crate or playpen when not supervised), and instead offered chew toys, he will most likely chew on them instead. Since chewing on the toy soothed this need to chew, it was reinforcing, so chewing on toys will continue. Eventually he will build a habit of chewing toys, and your table legs are saved. So, managing access to reinforcers to only ones that you provide is the first and most important step.

Tools: Baby Gates, Crates, Play Pens, Fences, and Leashes, are about restricting access to reinforcers that build "bad behaviors." (example: Finding food in the trash reinforces digging in the trash. A baby gate restricting access would prevent trash digging from being reinforced). Kongs, chew toys, tug ropes balls, interactive toys, and treats are for reinforcing behaviors that we want to build. (example: using a tug rope to teach the dog how to drop things he has in his mouth). I will be discussing particular tools as I explore each training topic.

Remember, any behavior that your dog continues to perform, good or bad, is being reinforced in some way. If you want to stop or prevent a behavior, you must figure out what is reinforcing it and restrict access to that reinforcer. Then you can build new acceptable, or desired, behaviors by reinforcing those. This is where training comes in.

Training

Exactly what is training, and why is it important? In short, training is opening a line of communication between the dog and its family. It's teaching the dog what we expect of him and adjusting our behavior in order to better communicate what we require.

We humans can sometimes be terrible communicators, especially when it comes to different species. Unfortunately in relation to dogs, this usually leads to manipulating them with force or intimidation until the dog figures out how to avoid it, and in the end we have a dog that seemingly listens and obeys our commands but may have developed some underlying issues that can crop up in the future as a result of this.

Fortunately, through science, we have learned better, healthier ways to communicate our needs that take into consideration the needs of the dog as well.

In the following pages you will learn some techniques that have been proven to be effective in teaching your dog how to perform behaviors on cue, or rather when we ask them to, but more importantly, they will show you the importance of why we teach them these cues and how they can help to prevent or change behaviors that we don't want.

Clicker / Marker Training

Before you begin training your dog tricks like sit, down, or spin, it is helpful teach your dog a clear signal that lets him know when he is correct. Reinforcement (treats, praise etc.) must happen within a second or so after the behavior in order for it to be paired with that behavior. So, asking for a sit, and then bumbling around your treat bag or going to the kitchen to retrieve a cookie from the treat jar, is ineffective. More than likely you have only reinforced following you into the kitchen or staring at your hand.

Charging the Marker

There are several ways of signaling your dog that he has earned reinforcement. A clicker is a noise-making device that can be used as such a signal. Other signals can be used as well such as a whistle, a hand gesture, or a marker word such as

"Yes." I personally prefer using the word "Yes," but sometimes I use the clicker. For clarity, from this point forward, I will refer to all of these signal makers as "Markers."

Whichever marker you choose, begin by first "charging" the marker by pairing it with reinforcement. This is one of the areas where classical conditioning is used. Start by simply using your marker and treating (i.e. click the clicker and immediately give the dog a treat, or say, "yes," and immediately give the dog a treat…). Wait a moment and repeat. Try to avoid marking while he is performing unwanted behaviors, or you run the risk of that behavior accidentally being trained. Continue marking following with a treat several times until you notice your dog quickly turning his attention to you when he hears the marker with excitement and anticipation. If it doesn't happen right away, don't worry. With some repetition, he will start to get it, given you are using a treat your dog really likes. Now you are ready to put it to use. Tip: Avoid marking without reinforcement, or you run the risk of weakening the marker's effectiveness.

This step is crucial to get right, and although it seems simple, I am told by new clients all the time that they have tried clicker training in the past, and it didn't work. In every case, it has been because they skipped this step, or didn't do it sufficiently enough that the marker had the emotional connection to the reinforcement that makes it such a powerful tool.

Easy as ABC

Later, I will describe how to train specific behaviors, but before we dive into that, it is necessary to understand a bit about the sequence of events when training any behavior.

ABC refers to the sequence of Antecedent, Behavior, Consequence, and it is the order of events that must occur in training to achieve the desired outcome.

1. Antecedent = What happens before the behavior. Most importantly, this refers to the "cue," but it also includes what hand gestures you are using,

where you are standing, what's going on around you, whether or not there other people or dogs present, how you are standing, and what has just happened. There are many other things you could possibly add to this list, but basically it's important to realize that it's not just what you say to the dog that affects behavior.

2. Behavior = What the dog does in response to the antecedent. When asked to sit, does he sit, or does he just stand there, wander off, or bark at you? It is the result of learning and is contingent on the consequence.

3. Consequence = What happens as a result of the behavior. Does he get reinforced? Is there punishment?

Understanding that these are connected as a loop can greatly progress training. Example: Although the Antecedent refers to what happens first in this sequence, the consequential history for the following behavior is an important part of the antecedent picture.

CHAPTER 3

Food

All dogs are motivated by food - some more than others. If they were not, they would die. Before domestication, dogs would spend a considerable part of their day scavenging, sniffing out prey, hunting, chasing, killing, dissecting, and eating their catch. It was a matter of life and death, and it is a survival instinct that is built into their DNA.

Now, thousands of years later, dogs have come to depend on us for their meals, and although unnecessary, those instincts still exist. For us this can be a good thing or a bad thing. Many of the normal dog behaviors that we humans see as "bad behavior," such as tearing up pillows, chasing cats, incessant sniffing on walks, and others, are directly related to this; and without an outlet for these behaviors, they can cause serious problems. On the positive side, we can use this to our advantage when training our dogs.

Throw away that food bowl! By placing their food in a bowl, putting it on the floor and walking away, you have just blown the best opportunity for modifying your dog's behavior. Since working for their food is built into their DNA, it is far healthier mentally for them to work to gain access to their food.

Use their food as training treats. Put their daily allowance of food in a ziplock baggie. If you usually feed twice a day, use those times to train. Keep in mind, training sessions should only last about 5 minutes, so If you have food left over, place it in a Kong, or scatter it in the grass, so they can continue to work for it. If you train using food, what better time to train than when they are hungry. This is not to suggest that you starve your dogs before training them. Just plan your training periods to coincide with feeding time.

Free feeding versus scheduled feeding times

One crucial thing to remember is that feeding your dog should always be done on a schedule. So whether you feed once, twice, or three times a day, it should be around the same time every day. And if the food is not consumed within about 20 minutes, it should be put away. This is helpful in many different ways. Here are a few:

1. It will help in potty training. If they eat on schedule, it's easier to predict when they need to go to the bathroom.

2. It makes training easier. As I said before, if your dog is hungry, it's much easier to train with food, so schedule training times during feeding times to optimize this reinforcer.

3. It helps to prevent finicky eaters. Most people who tell me their dog won't train for treats, free feed their

dogs. Once they start scheduling their feeding times, there is usually a tremendous change.

4. It helps to prevent resource guarding which is when dogs growl or snap at their owner for approaching their food bowl. If you have a dog that already does this, I recommend consulting with a certified professional dog trainer.

What should you feed your dog?
This can be a touchy subject, but my recommendation is that at the very least make sure the first ingredient in your dog's food is meat. If it's in the budget, I would recommend a grain-free food. It is much healthier, and your dog will poop less, so less clean up, and it helps with potty training. If your dog has allergy issues, try a limited ingredient dog food. A popular trend is a raw diet, which can be very expensive, but studies have shown it to be a very healthy option. In the end, I would suggest that you get the best you can afford.

Feeding your dog a healthy diet can be expensive, but in the end, it can even out. When you feed your dog a healthy diet, you don't have to feed as much, because they are getting more nutrients in the food you give them. It can also reduce your vet bills and help them to live long, happy lives. The way I see it, they are family members and deserve the best we can give them.

Treats in training

"Can I use treats instead of my dog's food to train?" Definitely, just be careful to not overfeed your dog. Try your best to determine the caloric intake of the treats, and reduce the amount of kibble you feed your dog by that much. Use small, healthy treats. I like to use real chicken, cut up to about the size of a pea. Why? Because healthy commercial dog treats are expensive. For a small 6 oz bag of healthy treats, you will spend approximately the same amount as you will on a 3 lb bag of frozen chicken tenders. Before a training session, just boil a chicken tender, and cut it up. If you have left overs, place it in the refrigerator for later. Remember that in the beginning stages of training, you should be using a high rate of reinforcement.

CHAPTER 4

Environmental Effects on Behavior

"Sit" means "Sit," right? Maybe not, at least not to your dog. You see it all the time, a dog parent out at the dog park telling their dog to sit over and over, getting louder as they go. "I don't understand, he does it so well at home," or even more common, "he's so stubborn." The problem is not that he's being stubborn, more likely it's that you have not taught him to sit at the park. Look at it this way, airline pilots don't just jump into the cockpit and start flying. First they must learn about the plane and how all the controls work. They spend hours upon hours in a flight simulator before ever leaving the ground. Eventually, they go up with a flight instructor for many more hours before sitting in that pilot seat. In the beginning, asking your dog to sit in the kitchen next to the treat jar can seem very different than asking them to sit in the hallway. So adding in distractions, like a park full of other dogs and people, can be like someone putting us in the pilot seat without any instruction, skills, or practice. To help your dog succeed, you should teach his cues in numerous locations, and conditions, with a variety of rewards. And practice, practice, practice. Make sure he is proficient in each location before changing. Each time you change locations, or some other environmental condition, back up your criteria for the behavior you are training. For example, you may have to shorten the duration you have your dog in a stay, so that it's easier for him to succeed when in a new location. Once he is successful at the shorter stay several times, you can gradually add duration. Remembering to do this with each new behavior will drastically reduce frustration for you and your dog. Eventually, he will generalize his behaviors to most environments.

Fear

One area where dogs seem to generalize all too well is fear and emotional responses. I volunteer as a behavior consultant at a local dog shelter, and one constant is dogs that have become reactive, aggressive, or just completely shut down due to poor socialization, abuse, or simply not helped to deal with something that made them nervous. Fear has a way of taking hold of a dog and completely controlling their lives, and sometimes all it takes is one bad experience to send them on a downward spiral.

The Critical Period

Several years ago I had a unique experience. A friend took me to see some deer that a man had in a pen in his backyard. There were several does and one really big buck. What amazed me is how tame they were. As we walked in the pen, they came walking up to us, nudging us as if to say they were happy to see us. I asked him how they came to be so relaxed around people. He told me that he had rescued them all as fawns. He had been around them their entire life, and as often as he was able, had invited people to come to see them. So why are deer in the wild so shy of people? Simple, because of lack of exposure to people during the first weeks of life. This is called "the critical period," and all animals, including humans, have it. It's in our DNA, and is part of a survival mechanism that helps to ensure the continuation of the species. During this period is when animals develop a sense of what is safe and what is unsafe in the world. Anything that they are not exposed to is considered unsafe, and although they can habituate to novel things later in life, it is much more difficult.

All the deer in this man's pen had positive exposure to humans during this period, so they perceived humans as friendly. Dogs have this same mechanism, and it is why it is so important to socialize them heavily the first twelve to sixteen weeks of their lives. Without socialization, dogs are far less confident, and will struggle with learning new things.

Fear Periods

Why has my dog all the sudden become afraid of the vacuum cleaner? Until dogs reach about two years of age, they go through something called fear periods. This is best described as periods where they suddenly become nervous about things they seemingly were fine with before. It is very important that you don't ignore this. Dr. Ian Dunbar, a world-renowned trainer and veterinarian behaviorist, says you should never expect behavior to stay the same. Fear will generally get worse unless you intercede. To help your dog through these periods, use lots of calm reassurance. Make sure you are not adding to the problem by getting amped up yourself. Use treats. Food releases endorphins, a chemical that is related to good feelings. If you pair scary stimuli with treats, presenting the treat immediately after the stimuli, eventually the stimuli will take on a new meaning. Vacuum = treats. It is imperative to deal with fear issues right away. Fear has a way of spiraling out of control. If your dog is struggling with nervousness or fear, I strongly recommend that you seek the help of a professional Behavior Consultant.

Avoiding Fear in Training

Since fear can be so debilitating, I always try to be as cautious as possible when training to not scare the dog with big gestures, a loud voice, or in some cases, a lot of direct eye contact in the beginning. With some dogs, something as small as the way you walk into the room can have a dramatic effect on them, especially if they already have issues.

As you are training watch the dog. Is he backing away, are his ears flat against his head, is his tail tucked? These are a few of the obvious signs that he may not be ok with the situation. There are many others, and familiarizing yourself with a dog's body language is very beneficial. There are some good resources online about the subject. One being barkpost.com which has some great charts that show how to interpret certain body language.

Unfortunately, many trainers still purposefully use fear and intimidation in training. There is no denying its effectiveness; however, you need to ask yourself at what cost. Although many dogs seem bomb proof, and can handle the effects of this aversive method of training, many shut down to the point of barely being able to function. And I would argue that even those "bomb-proof dogs" are affected in ways that may not be apparent now,
but may come back to haunt them down the road.

Test your knowledge

1. You pick up a leash every day prior
    to waking your dog. After a few days,
    she gets excited and runs to the door
    every time you grab the leash. What is
    this called?
    A. Operant conditioning
    B. Classical conditioning
    C. Food conditioning

2. Your dog makes an association
    between something she does and the
    consequence. This is called?
    A. Operant conditioning
    B. Consequential conditioning
    C. Classical conditioning

3. In behavioral science, positive and
    negative means?
    A. Good and bad
    B. The opposite ends of a battery
    C. To add or remove something

4. Your dog gets a treat for sitting, so he
    learns that sitting equals treats. This is
    called?

A. Negative reinforcement
B. Positive training
C. Positive reinforcement

5. What is a marker?
   A. An ink dispensing device
   B. A signal that lets the dog know that reinforcement is available
   C. Something that shows the dog where to go

6. In the phrase "consequence drives behavior," what is a consequence?
   A. A treat when the dog sits
   B. A jerk on the leash when the dog pulls
   C. A snack when the dog digs in the trash
   D. All of the above

7. In dog training (behavioral science) ABC refers to?
   A. Antecedent, Behavior, Consequence
   B. The Alphabet song
   C. Act before consequence

8. What is the best way to feed your dog?
    A. With scheduled feedings
    B. By leaving the food down all the time
    C. When he asks for it

9. What is a major factor to consider when you ask your dog to perform a task?
    A. What time of day it is
    B. Where you are
    C. What other dogs are in the area
    D. All of the above

10. Your puppy is scared of other people. What should you do?
    A. Nothing, he will grow out of it
    B. Force him to be handled by strangers
    C. Offer him treats and calm reassurance in the presents of strangers

11. Socializing means?
    A. Letting your puppy get to know the family and other family dogs only
    B. Taking him to doggy day care
    C. Letting him have a many positive experiences with other people, dogs and novel things as possible

12. Your 6 month old dog suddenly becomes scared of the vacuum cleaner. What is this a symptom of?
    A. Fear period
    B. Critical period
    C. Trauma period

13. Treating your dog each time he gets it right is an example of?
    A. Good training
    B. Continuous reinforcement
    C. Variable reinforcement

14. What is an example of reinforcement?
    A. Treats
    B. Pets and praise
    C. Play
    D. Access to environments
    E. All of the above

Answers: 1. C 2. A 3. C 4. C 5. B 6. D
7. A 8. A 9. D 10. C 11. C 12. A 13. B
14. E

CHAPTER 5

So You Got a Dog, What Now?

Puppies

Mommy, where do puppies come from?

Children are great at asking uncomfortable questions. I'll leave how you answer that question up to you, but making good choices about where, or rather what breeder, to purchase your beloved pup from, can go a long way in ensuring you end up with a well-behaved, healthy pup. The more you know about the breeder, the environment in which the puppies are kept, and what the puppies parents are like, the better. Of course, once you have your pup, all of that is mute.

Now it's up to you to mold your pup into the adult dog you want him to be regardless of the difficulties or limitations put in place by genetics or poor postnatal care.

Socialization

I have discovered that when it comes to socialization, everyone seems to have a different idea as to what this word means. Most pet owners I have worked with have the idea that socialization means letting the pup get acquainted with the family, and maybe a couple of family dogs. However, this is really just scratching the surface. The first 12 to 16 weeks of your pup's life are the most critical in terms of helping him to be confident. This is when he learns what is safe, and unsafe, in the world. The more positive experiences he can have with other humans and dogs, the better. So take him out, and let him see the world. Just make sure you are there when he needs you to help him work through things that make him nervous. This can be done by attending puppy socialization classes; however, there are risks to this method, number one being parvo. Before attending class, your pup should have his first vaccinations. This is not going to protect him from the parvovirus, but most veterinary behaviorists believe that the risk of antisocial behavior trumps this concern. Far more dogs are put down every year due to poor social skills than the parvovirus.

Other less risky options are: 1. Invite friends over to meet your pup. People with beards, people that wear hats, skirts, and glasses. You can even have them play dress up in all kinds of crazy costumes. 2. Take your pup to pet-friendly stores like Home Depot, Lowes, Michaels, Tractor Supply, and Atwoods.

There are many others. You would need to research what's available in your community. I would suggest doing this during a slow time in the store so that your pup doesn't get overwhelmed. If at any point he appears overly stressed, leave and try a less scary environment until he gains more confidence.

People are drawn to puppies like a magnet. If they ask to pet your pup, first look to see if he is interested in interacting with the stranger. If he seems excited to meet them, give the stranger a treat, and ask them to feed it to your puppy before petting him. Save extra special treats for children as they tend to move erratically and can make your puppy nervous.

For dog interactions, having play dates with friends and family dogs, or joining a dog socialization group, are some good options. You can find lots of dog groups on social media, and plan play dates. When meeting other puppies, make sure they are current on their shots, and appear healthy and energetic. Do not force interaction. If your pup seems nervous, give him a place to escape, such as under your legs or in a play pen. Let him approach the other pup on his terms and in his own time. If the other puppy invades his space, and your pup appears overly nervous, remove the invader. Make sure your pup feels like it can come to you for safety and comfort. Eventually, you may find your pup becoming curious about the other pup. If the pups begin playing, supervise closely, and if either pup gets overly excited, or gets overly aggressive in his play, pick him up and walk away for a short time out. Give them about 10 seconds apart, and then let them continue playing. Repeat this as often as necessary.

Once you have dogs, and people, covered, you need to be creative. Make a list of anything novel you think your dog may come in contact with that may make him nervous, and gently expose him to the stimuli. Keep treats with you, and pair each new thing with treats. Keep the treats hidden until the stimulus appears, and instantly make the food appear. When the stimulus is removed, put the treats away. Some examples would be bicycles, vacuum cleaners, balloons, cars, motorcycles, wheelchairs, and crutches.

In addition, exposing them to husbandry procedures is crucial. Think of anything a vet, groomer, or child would do, and gently expose your pup to similar experiences. Gently tugging on his ears, tail, and fur, opening his mouth and touching his teeth, spreading his toes and pulling on his toenails are all examples of things you can try. Pair them all with treats, only revealing them directly after the stimulus, and then putting them away. Go slow and gentle with this, and soon you'll have a pup that looks forward to these procedures.

Immunization

One of the most important things you can do for your pup is to stay current on their shots. Not just for the health of the pup, but for everyone around him as well. Many of the diseases these vaccines prevent can be transferred to humans, and some can be fatal. For this reason, the first thing you should do when your pup comes home is make an appointment with your veterinarian.

What's special about your pup?

When you select a new puppy it's very important that you consider what kind of dog he will be. You should also consider where you live, your lifestyle, and if the breed is suited to those conditions. That cute little husky pup may seem like a good idea, after all who wouldn't love snuggling up to a little ball of fluff? But that pup will soon grow up, and if you live in a small apartment, you're in for a world of hurt. Huskies were bred to pull sleds. They have tremendous energy and stamina, and keeping them in a small apartment without an outlet for that energy is a recipe for disaster. Destruction of furniture, walls, windows, and personal items is common in situations like this; and in many cases, training alone will not solve the problem. Examples like this are way too common, and are one of the biggest reasons dogs end up in shelters. On the other hand, if you choose a dog that is appropriate for the situation, he can be one of the greatest gifts life has to offer. So do your homework before bringing a puppy home, and your life, and his, will be much more pleasant.

What do I do now?

What do you do If you made the wrong decision and brought a pup home that's not appropriate for your
lifestyle? In a word, the best you can. When you bring a dog home, it is your responsibility to keep him healthy and happy. Training and management (crates, baby gates, and playpens), along with healthy food and exercise, can go a long way toward making this journey easier. Don't forget, it's not the dog's fault. He is simply displaying behavior he was bred for.

What's good for the dog

In the end, if you have tried your best and nothing is working, you have to consider the welfare of the dog, and if keeping

him is in his best interest. It's difficult
to consider rehoming your dog. It feels
like you have failed him, but sometimes
forcing him to live in a situation that does
not suit him can be detrimental to him.
We need to always remind ourselves that
we chose this relationship, so we are
responsible for his happiness even if that
means finding him a better place to live.

Adult Dogs

Choosing the right dog for you

When you get a new adult dog, there are
a lot of things to consider before, and
immediately after, you bring him home,
to ensure successful integration into your
family. Below is a list of 10 questions you
should ask yourself, and some tips for a
smooth transition.

1.   Is your new dog from a shelter?

It's heart-wrenching to see those sweet
faces behind bars. If I followed my heart,
I would take every one of them home.

Of course, that would be impossible, but just maybe one... or two... or ok, maybe three. My point is that it's very hard to think clearly, and realistically, when you're in the heat of the moment, but If your end goal is to give the dog you choose the best life you can offer, you have to set some boundaries. Most shelter dogs have been through a lot. The shelter that they are in may seem like a scary, stressful place for a dog, but it may also be the first stable place they have ever lived. When you rescue a dog from a shelter, you have to consider that he may come with a lot of baggage, some of which you may not be prepared to deal with. Many dogs that are rescued end up right back in that same shelter. That is, if they are lucky, and not just dropped off on the side of the road somewhere. I'm not suggesting that you don't rescue, but it's imperative that you do your homework and find out as much as possible about the dog you are considering. Ask the volunteers, who walk and feed them every day, what they are like, how they came to be at the shelter, and how long they have been there.

Then consider if you are the appropriate caregiver for that particular dog.

2.   What's his temperament?

This is kind of a vague question that harbors many other questions like: Is he a laid-back couch potato? Is he high energy? Does he have a strong "prey drive?" Does he have a strong need to work? Or how has his breeding affected how he responds to any stimuli in his environment? Having an answer to these questions is important. There is possibly a home for all of these examples, but should it be yours? How does your lifestyle match up?

3.   What is his personality?

Although breed and temperament are important considerations, there is more to the story. When choosing an adult dog, I would argue that it is not the most important factor. You may have heard the phrase nature vs nurture. Nature refers to the temperament of the dog, which is the role genetics plays in shaping the dog, and nurture refers to the personality of the dog which is the role that those genes, plus experiences/the environment, have had on the dog. When choosing a dog for your family, both should be considered; however, how the dog has been raised should carry more weight. Many breeds have been written off by some. They deem them dangerous or aggressive, and while it is true that dogs are a product of their DNA, there is more to them than the sum of their parts. They forget the tremendous role environment has on them. Breeds like Pit Bulls, Rottweilers, and German Shepherds get labeled as aggressive when the vast majority are sweet, gentle, family dogs. Their DNA may include tendencies that make them protective, or more sensitive to certain stimuli, but it is the environment that teaches them what is safe and unsafe, and what reaction from them works to deal with that stimuli. In a nutshell, when choosing a new dog, you should consider its breed and temperament; but, more importantly, how he has been raised, has there been any training, was there any abuse, and how resilient he is. Then ask yourself if you are prepared to help your new dog work through any of the baggage he may have. What's your game plan for managing him until he has been shown the ropes?

4. What's your new dog's age?

Dogs of all ages are amazing creatures, but the differences in old dogs and young dogs are significant. Obviously, the dog you choose is going to age and change while in your care, but choosing a dog for where you are at present will go a long way in making the transition go smoothly. So what age is appropriate for your lifestyle?

Adolescent dogs usually have boundless energy, and if they have not been taught some impulse control, can be quite a handful. But if you have time, and energy to match, I say go for it. The vast number of dogs in shelters fit into this category for the very reasons I expressed above.

It is a myth that you can't teach an old dog new tricks. Many older dogs get looked over at shelters because people think they would be difficult, and too set in their ways, but older dogs can definitely be trained using positive reinforcement training, and they are usually so sweet and loving. However, older dogs generally have more health problems, and veterinary bills can sometimes add up quickly.

5.   What sex, and is your new dog spayed or neutered? Just like with humans, males and females act differently especially when it comes to their sex drive. Although I encourage all pet owners to have their dogs fixed, in the case of male dogs, it can sometimes have a significant effect on their behavior. It can sometimes help with marking, mild reactivity, and roaming; however, new studies have shown, if the surgery is performed too early, it can have a negative effect on aggressive tendencies. I would suggest holding out until they are around a year old if possible.

Another area where the sex of your dog is an important consideration is when you have multiple dogs. It is usually best to have dogs of the opposite sex, especially if you have two female dogs. They tend to have more disagreements than two males as long as the males are neutered.

6. Do you have other dogs or cats? It's often thought that it's better to have two dogs so that they can keep each other company when you're away. Usually, it's a dog owner that has a dog that has become destructive when they are away, so to help the dog with bad behavior attributed to boredom, they get another dog. While this sometimes works great, there are a few things you need to consider.

-   How will your dog feel about another dog in your house? Although he may be perfectly fine to meet other dogs out in public, sharing resources can be a very different thing.

- How does your dog's energy level compare to the new dog's energy level? If you end up with two high strung dogs, instead of solving your problem, it's possible you may just end up with twice the destructive behaviors.

- What is their age difference? If you have an older dog, and you bring in a new puppy with tons of energy, it can be very frustrating to your dog, and sometimes even the sweetest dog can be pushed to his limit and lash out.

- Is there a significant size difference? I have a GSD and a Miniature Dachshund, and I have to confess that I am constantly worried about my little girl getting hurt. Don't get me wrong, they are the best of friends, but they sometimes play so rough (usually instigated by my dachshund), and I know all it would take is one little mishap, and we would be off to the vet. We've been very lucky so far. She's a tough little thing.

- Don't forget, two dogs mean twice the training time, feeding time, cleaning time, and grooming time.

7. Do you have children? Children can be very scary to dogs. Especially if they are very young. They move weird, can be noisy, and sometimes handle them roughly. This can all lead to disaster if you are not cautious. It is important to let your dog have a "safe space" where they can go to get away from children, and your children need to be taught that when they are in that space, they are off limits. If you have a very young child, this may need to be in a crate, or behind a gate, so they can't reach them; and even still, the children need to be supervised, so they never tease the dog while in their safe space. Make sure all interactions with the dog are closely supervised, and if either is getting too rough, they should be separated.

8. Is he crate trained, and where will he sleep? Crate training a new dog, in my opinion, is one of the best things you can do for your dog. I'm not suggesting using a crate to store your dog away until you want to play with him, but if you're going to be gone, it's important to make it easy for him to be successful in your absence until he learns the rules. I will discuss strategies later.

9. How much time will he be alone? Dogs are social animals. They have been bred for thousands of years to have a desire to work and live around humans - especially some breeds. It is extremely unfair to get a dog and expect him to spend 10 hours a day in a crate, to then be let outside only to be ignored until bedtime, then placed back into the crate. I understand that we have to work, but there are options like hiring a dog walker, coming home at lunch to let him out, or doggy daycare. Letting your dog outside to self-exercise is not enough.

They need interaction and mental stimulation. Imagine being kept in a tiny room with nothing to do all day. I, for one, would go stir crazy. This is possibly the most important thing to consider before getting a dog.

10. Do you have time to train him? Management can only go so far, and who wants to constantly be concerned that your dog is going to act inappropriately. Making time to show your dog how to survive in a world where normal dog behavior is sometimes not acceptable is only fair. Imagine if you suddenly lived in a world that normal human behaviors were unacceptable. Then imagine that no one told you the rules, but punished you if you broke them. What a difficult scenario, but we ask dogs to do this all the time. Hopefully, if you are reading this, you realize that, and I applaud you. If this method of training doesn't work for you, I encourage you to find one that does. It's the humane thing to do.

Bringing a new do g home.

Bringing a new dog home can be a challenging experience, especially with an adult dog you've rescued or adopted from the shelter. Previously I spoke of management, and while this should be in place before bringing a new dog home, beyond that, there are a few other procedures that should be followed to ensure that your dog adjusts to its new environment, and to any people or other pets in that environment.

Procedure for introducing your new dog to your other dogs

1. Introduce them off-site. Let them meet at a park or other neutral territory. With them on leash, begin by walking them parallel to one another at a distance where they can see one another. Slowly drift closer and further away a few times until they appear relaxed around one another. In a way, you want to let your dogs choose how close, or how far, the distance is, but if they are pulling toward one

another in a straight line, in a way that their bodies are aligned, and they are staring each other down, spread a little further apart and continue walking. Don't rush this. You want them to meet but you don't want to force it. **Never pull them toward one another.**

2. Once you are close enough for them to possibly meet, try to keep a loose leash, and look for friendly greeting signs such as play bows, open mouths, relaxed ears, loose curved bodies, and a neutral or low wagging tail. Keep the greeting very short (5 seconds) then call them away. Try to avoid pulling on the leash unless you have to, as this can cause stress and possibly cause your dog to react. Try luring them away with a treat instead. As they walk away, give them a high-value treat, and after a short rest, let them meet again. Once you have them together, stay on the outside, and as they circle, follow them around so the leashes don't get tangled. Do this several times before letting them

spend more time together. Make sure that you have equipment for breaking up a fight on hand just in case, like Pet Safe spray, a blanket, or a water bottle.

3. Move it to the yard. If they did well, greeting on leash a few times at the park, try letting them meet off leash in the yard. Make sure you supervise this, preferably with two or more people present, but don't crowd them. Again, keep equipment to break up a potential fight on hand. Let them have plenty of space to escape if they choose to. Call them apart often, and reward them with praise if they come.

4. Time to go inside. If all goes well outdoors, let the new dog come into the house without your other dog, so that he can have some time sniffing around. This will help him to relax and feel a bit more comfortable with his new home before bringing in your other dog. It's best if your other dog is off-site when this happens, so that he

doesn't see your new dog go in. After some time, take him back out into the yard. Now try bringing them both in, but let the new dog enter first. Try to give them plenty of space. Call them out of any tight spaces before arousal goes up. Make sure all food, beds, and toys are put away before bringing the dogs in.

Introducing family members

1. When you bring your dog home, keep it low key. Your children will be excited, so discuss with them ahead of time the importance of being calm and quiet.

2. Don't crowd your new dog. Give him space to explore and sniff.

3. Let him approach family members. Wait for your dog to greet them rather than them approaching him. Keep petting short, and don't pat but rather stroke or scratch slowly.

4. Don't pet him on top of the head or hug him. This is especially important for children to understand.

5. Don't invite people over for a couple of weeks. Let him have a chance to get used to his new surroundings before adding new things or people.

6. Don't go to the dog park for at least a month. Personally, I am not a fan of dog parks. They are a huge gamble. Your dog may be well behaved, but you never know about the other dogs at the park. I prefer going to a park where all the dogs are leashed. If you want to let your dogs interact with other well behaved dogs, consider having play dates with friends dogs or join a training class.

7. Make sure all interaction with children is supervised, and remind them of the rules often.

Create a safe space

1. Your new dog needs to have a place to get away from children, other dogs, and you. A crate is a great way to do this. (see the section on crate training)

2. Some dogs may have anxiety issues and may not do well in a crate. For those, a gated kitchen, or another dog-safe room, may be better, or you can use an exercise pen or playpen. Feed all of their meals in this space, and have bedding for them to sleep. Children need to know this space is off limits when the dog is in it.

Let your new dog know you have his back.

Below are some ways you can help your dog acclimate to his new home and feel that you are are looking out for him.

1. Scheduled feeding times away from other dogs in a calm relaxed space. All food should be put up 15 to 20 minutes after you put it down. This

goes for all dogs in the house. If your old dog is a grazer, this needs to change. Present the food to your dogs. Ask them to eat. You may need to add a little incentive for a couple of days like canned food, low sodium chicken or beef stock, or yogurt to the top of their bowl. After the allotted time remove the food. After a few meal times, your dog should begin to get it.

2. Regular hourly bathroom breaks to the same place in the yard, with you present, will help with potty training; and since dogs can feel vulnerable when using the bathroom, your presence may help him feel safe, as long as you never punish him for accidents in the house. Note: some shelter dogs may have a history of being punished when they had an accident. In this case, give him plenty of space, but watch from a distance, and reward as soon as he is finished.

3. Scheduled walks will burn off excess energy that may otherwise be used in destructive ways, and can help your

dog feel more comfortable with his new surroundings. The interaction and direction from you will go a long way in helping him learn how you communicate, and the alone time will help him bond with you.

4.   Set him up to succeed by keeping him confined to his "safe space" when you are away.

Let your old dog know that the new dog is not a threat.

1.   Give extra attention to the dog you already had (Rover).

2.   Spend time alone with him.

3.   Show him that the presence of the new dog (Fido) is beneficial to him by rewarding him with treats when you pet or give Fido attention.

4.   If Rover was previously allowed on the furniture, continue to allow him there. Only allow Fido on the furniture after he has been there a couple of

weeks, and there is lots of space, so you can be between the dogs. Or have someone else call Fido up to sit by them as you reward Rover. When he approaches the couch, ask him up, when he jumps up, watch Rover. If he remains in place give him a treat, or just pet and tell him he's a good boy if you think Fido will invade his space to try to get the treat.

Outside play time

Giving the dogs time to be together outdoors, in a fenced yard, is a great way to let them bond. Just make sure they are supervised the entire time in case over-excited play becomes too aggressive. Take lots of breaks, and keep it fun.

CHAPTER 6

Let the training begin

Crate Training

To many people the idea of using a crate conjures up images like the one here. They are concerned that they are being cruel to their dog if they put them in a crate, and to be fair, if the dog is not trained properly, or is left in the crate for excessively long periods of time, it can be cruel.

But in the same right, teaching a dog to use a kennel, or crate, is one of the most valuable things you can teach them. It prevents a whole host of problem behaviors from being rehearsed. It makes potty training a snap and gives them a safe space to relax away from things, or people, that may create stress. Most dogs learn to enjoy their crate. There are lots of different methods for teaching this behavior. Below is one that I have found to be the easiest and most effective.

1. Bedtime is too late. Practice going into and getting used to the crate several times before you actually need them to be in there.

2. Make the crate comfy. Place a towel or blanket on the floor of the crate, and maybe one under the crate, to dampen the sound of the plastic hitting the floor when your dog walks on it. They are sometimes quite noisy and may startle your pup.

3.   Is it safe? Set up your crate in a room where the family gathers. Most dogs are curious and will want to go sniff it. Tie the door open with a bungee cord, or piece of string, so that if your dog goes in, they won't accidentally bump the door causing it to swing open or shut. This could startle them and get off on a bad foot.

4.   What's in it for me? Reward any interest by giving your dog a treat when they approach or sniff the kennel. If they go inside, reward extra.

5.   Place several treats inside the crate and watch. If they go in, "mark," and let them eat the treats. Once they have finished, call them out of the crate, and wait to see if they go back in to investigate. When they go in, "mark," and drop a treat in from the top. Repeat this step until they are quickly going back in after being called out.

6.   Once they are repeating the behavior regularly, add the cue "kennel up"

just as they are heading back into the kennel. Continue to do this several times. Then try saying the cue just before they turn to go back into the kennel. If they go in, mark, treat, and repeat.

7. Some dogs may be nervous about the mere presence of the kennel. If this is the case, try tossing treats toward the entrance, and then away from the entrance. If you only get closer to the door, the dog may figure out that you're luring him in. Make it a game of "find the treat." Eventually, toss the treat just inside the door. When he gets it, throw another one outside the crate. Repeat this several times until he appears comfortable with the crate. Then just before tossing the treat in, say "kennel up". Pretend to toss the treat in, and if he goes after it, mark, and toss in the treat.

8. Once they are going in regularly, continue to toss treats in while they are inside the crate, so that they start

spending more time inside. You can
also hide several treats inside folds in
the towel, or blanket, so that they will
have to search for them.

9. Feed all meals inside the crate. With
the dog waiting just outside the crate,
place their dinner in a bowl, put it
inside the crate, and close the door.
Wait a few seconds so that your dog
builds up a desire to get to the food.
Say "kennel up," and open the door.
Do this at each meal time, and let
them eat their entire meal inside the
crate.

After you have done this a few times,
hold the food bowl near the door,
and say the cue, before you put the
food bowl in. They will most likely
go in immediately. When they go in,
place the food bowl in the kennel. As
they are eating, gently push the door
closed, but don't latch it. Allow them to
push it open if they choose.

10. Make sure the cue retains value.
Make sure that you don't overuse the

Kennel Up cue. If they don't go in after the first cue, encourage them with body language, and if necessary lure them with the food. Soon they should start going in when they hear the cue.

11. Shutting the door. Practice saying the cue and tossing a treat in when they enter. As they find their treat, close and latch the door for a few seconds, and then let them out. As you open the door, give a release cue like "OK," and let them out. Repeat several times, and slowly add duration before you open the door. Make sure that you occasionally reduce the duration as well. Try to avoid waiting so long that they start whining and pawing at the door.

12. Add distance. When you first start closing the door, you should stay right beside the crate. You can also drop treats in through the top of the crate to add to the length of time they are in the crate, but once you have built up some duration, start stepping away and returning, dropping a treat at each

return. First, just a few steps, then five, then ten, and so on, rewarding on each return.

13. Leaving the room. Once your dog is successful at duration and distance, practice stepping out of sight for a few seconds, and then return to reinforce silence. Continue adding duration while out of sight, being careful not to push your dog too hard. It is much easier to reach your end goal if your dog is successful at every step before moving on.

14. Building a habit. After you have practiced the above sequence for a few sessions, start putting your dog in the kennel for short periods all throughout the day while you use the restroom, fold laundry, or eat dinner. Keep chew toys in the kennel, so he will have something to occupy his time while in the crate. A Kong stuffed with tasty treats is a great tool for this.

15. Spending the night. Once he is staying for short periods successfully,

it's time to let him spend the night. Just be sure to keep water available, and let him out to use the bathroom. If he starts whimpering, don't let him out unless he is becoming distressed, and try to wait for a lull of a few seconds in the whining before opening the kennel.

16. A tired dog is a happy dog. Don't forget to exercise your dog before putting him in the kennel for any significant time. Expecting a dog that is full of energy to lie quietly for hours in a confined space is just unrealistic and unfair.

Potty Training

Probably the most searched topic in regards to puppies on the internet, and yet one of the simplest behaviors to train, is housebreaking.

Remember the golden rule, "consequence drives behavior?" Well, it bears repeating. If using the bathroom outside is beneficial, then it's going to continue. It's not only true for the dog, its true for us too. Think about it, if we just went to the bathroom anywhere we got the urge, it would be disgusting, right? So we, without exception, do our business in the bathroom. Most dogs, if able, will not go to the potty where they sleep. They prefer to keep that area clean and comfy. So if we use a crate to confine the dog, they will most likely not go there, so we add a bit of predictability into the equation. That is as long as we don't make them wait too long.

So where else can we find some predictability? It's a given that puppies are going to need to potty after they eat. If we schedule feeding times two to three times a day, always at the same time, and keep food put away after mealtime, we will have two to three daily planned bathroom breaks shortly after each meal.

Some other predictors are play and sleep. Making sure to take them out immediately after play, and after they wake up from naps, will most assuredly result in success in the yard.

So now that we know when pups are most likely to go, it's
up to us to be consistent on our end. Beyond this, you should plan on taking them out every 45 minutes to an hour between these scheduled potty breaks. Of course, there is always the unpredictable, sudden need to go to consider. Sometimes, no matter how consistent we are, the sudden squat on the carpet is inevitable. So how do we deal with that? First, keep in mind that it's still on us to keep an ever-watching eye on our pups. If they are not in their crate, they should be constantly supervised. Blocking them in the room with you, putting them in a playpen, or tethering them to you, or near you, so they can't wander off to do their business, will help your dog to succeed. This is not only true for potty training, but also for lots of other inappropriate behaviors they may learn while exploring on their own.

Now that we know how to prevent going in the wrong place, how do we make them want to go in the right place? Did someone say "consequence drives behavior?" When you take your pup outside to potty, make sure you take them on a leash to the same spot each time. Once they do their business, mark and treat. Immediately! Don't wait till you go back inside to reward them. They won't make the connection between the reward and the act. Be extra exuberant! Make them think it's the greatest thing in the world to go to the bathroom outside. This means lots of great treats, and spending a few minutes in the yard, playing with them after they go potty. Most puppies love the chance to explore the great outdoors. If you immediately take them in after they do their business, they will start taking longer and longer to go, because they don't want to go back inside. They may even hold it, so they can play, and then when you give up and take them inside, they will go. Remember the predictor that puppies need to go immediately after play? Now you've essentially shown them that outside is the play area, and when you come back in is when you take care of business. Another thing to consider is that if you take them in immediately after they go, you are essentially punishing them for peeing outside. The act of pottying means the end of play time.

"But my dog takes forever." You can actually help speed things up. When you take your dog out, say nothing. Be as boring as you can be. When you see your dog circling or beginning to squat, and would bet money that they are going to go, say "go potty." Your timing has to be great. Say it once, and wait. When they are finished, reward with treats and play. Soon your dog will connect this cue with going to the bathroom, and you will be able to say it before they start squatting to cue him to go. If you say it too early, in the beginning, your dog will not understand what you are trying to communicate. The cue needs to predict the inevitable potty behavior.

So what do you do when accidents happen? In a word, nothing. You wouldn't scold an infant child for pottying in their diaper. Remember your dog's brain is much smaller than ours. We should never assume that they understand how things work. Punishing them for going in the house is just plain cruel, and it can actually backfire on you. Many times people will start noticing that their puppy will start sneaking off to do their business behind the couch or in another room. This is usually because they have been punished. It's not because they are being spiteful or vindictive, but rather they have decided that peeing in front of humans is unsafe, so they sneak off to a safe place where there are no humans. This problem extends to the yard. If your dog deems it unsafe to do their business around you, think about how they must feel if they are on a leash where they can't escape. Much better to wait till you're not around. So going behind the couch continues. This is true even if you find it later and punish them. Remember the consequence has to immediately follow the action for the two to be paired.

If you catch your dog in the act. Say STOP loudly, but not angrily, just to break their focus. This will sometimes stop the flow temporarily until you can pick them up and take them outside. Once they go, praise them, and reward them with treats and play. Make sure you clean the spot thoroughly with a cleaner specifically made to remove pet odors. Even if you can't smell it, it doesn't mean that they can't, and dogs will usually go where they have gone before. I like to suggest to my clients to roll up any rugs you may have until your dog has learned to go outside. Most dogs prefer to pee on grass, and sometimes rugs can be mistaken for it. It's also much harder to remove odors from rugs, so your dog will likely return for a repeat performance.

Consistency is the key to successful potty training. It's helpful for everyone in the family to be involved. Just make sure everyone is following the same game plan.

CHAPTER 7

Ten Most Common Obedience Cues

Quick note: the techniques shown below are ones that I have found to be the most effective on the majority of dogs; however, every dog is an individual, and in some cases, may require alternative methods.

Teaching Your Dog's Name
https://youtu.be/ZiPeTr65XLw

Teaching your dog to respond to his name, and how to keep their focus on you, is the foundation of all good training. To teach your dogs name, hold a treat in each hand above, and to the sides, of your dogs head. Say his name once in an exciting way. Watch closely. If he cuts his eyes to your face, even for a split second, mark and treat. Repeat several times. As he gets better, ask for longer eye contact before reinforcement. Caution: make sure you're quick with the marker. If you mark as your dog looks away, you will have reinforced looking away. If you are having difficulty getting your dog to look at your face, try holding the treat in your hand. Say his name, and raise the treat up between your eyes. When his eyes meet yours, mark and treat. When your dog has been successful several times in several short sessions, practice saying his name at random times throughout the day. Reward each time he is successful. If he does not look at you, don't make the mistake of repeating his name over and over. This will cause your dog to start ignoring his name. Instead, move closer, and this may cause him to look toward you. As he is turning his head, say his name. When he looks at you, mark and treat. If this does not work, go back to the beginning, and practice up close. Never call his name if you are going to punish him. This may also cause him to start ignoring his name.

If you are ever in the position where you feel it necessary for punishment, always go to him rather than calling him to you. It is very important to protect this behavior once you have taught it.

How to train Targeting
https://youtu.be/fB7Jii_f4X0

Targeting is an incredibly useful behavior used to move your dog through space. Not the outer kind, of course, but rather from one point to another. It involves having your dog touch his nose, or another body part, to your hand or a targeting stick. You can use this behavior to teach your dog to heel, get in the car, get in the crate, get off the couch, recall, and many other behaviors that require movement. One of the more important things it does is it allows you to have a more efficient training session. For example, if you teach your dog to sit, or down, it's important that you are able to get him back up quickly, so that you can repeat the behavior. So, after the sit, or down, you can ask him to touch your hand, causing him to have to get up.

It helps to teach behaviors in groups of 3 or more, so you can randomize the order in which you ask for behaviors. This prevents them from learning behaviors as part of a pattern. It is very common to see dogs that automatically go to a down when asked to sit, because the handler has practiced the two behaviors back to back, so the dog just skips a step and goes to what he perceives is the final behavior. Having the dog target your hand works nicely as a third behavior that you can add to the sit and down behaviors to keep your dog guessing which one is coming next. This will help him wait for the cue and respond correctly.

To teach targeting, hold both hands behind your back. Have a treat in one hand and nothing in the other hand. Present your empty hand very close to your dog's nose. The motion will attract him, and he should bump his nose to your hand. The moment his nose touches, mark, and treat. Repeat several times very close to his nose, and when he seems to get the concept, begin putting distance between your hand and his nose in small increments. Make sure he is proficient at each distance before adding more. After you have added a little distance, put your hand out, and when the dog moves, move your hand back so that he follows it, and eventually let him touch it. After he is able to do the behavior well, add the cue "touch" as you stick your hand out. When he touches it, mark, and treat.

Make a game out of it. Practice moving him all around the room, rewarding him each time he touches it with treats, play, and praise. Be animated. Once he is following your hand around, start moving erratically around the room. Running from spot to spot and presenting your hand. Have your dog follow your hand through your legs, and on and off of furniture. The goal is to make your dog enjoy bumping your hand. It also creates a kind of attachment to you where the dog is fixated and excited about your presence. This is useful in lots of training scenarios, especially loose leash walking, and working around distractions.

How to train Sit
https://youtu.be/HgKgTljl6WU

To teach sit, position your dog in front of you. Hold a treat in your hand with your palm up. Present the treat to your dogs nose, and slowly raise the treat up and back over his head. Remember to keep the treat close to his nose as you move it over his head, like the treat and his nose are two magnets. As his head goes back, his bottom should go down. If it doesn't happen immediately, wait a few seconds. With his head back, it is more comfortable to be in a sitting position, so he will most likely sit. The instant his bottom touches the floor, mark, and treat.

At this point you are not adding the cue or command. Repeat the step above a few more times. If he appears to be sitting faster, try removing the treat, and just use an empty hand to lure him. if he sits, mark, and reward from your other hand. Continue this step several more times without the treat in your luring hand. This has now become a hand signal, or prompt, for the dog to sit.

After he has become proficient at this, add the cue "Sit" one second before the hand signal. Mark, and treat. After you have done this several times, you will notice that he will start preempting the hand signal after he hears the cue to sit. At this point you can fade out the hand signal if you choose; however, if at any point he does not sit after the cue, use the hand signal rather than repeating the cue. Try to avoid putting your hand on the dogs bottom to force him down.

How to train Down
https://youtu.be/0PE5-ml3Pb8

Down should be taught from both the standing and sitting positions. Many find it easier to start from a sit position, so I will begin there.

With your dog in a sit, hold a treat in your hand with your palm down. Present it to your dog's nose, and slowly lower it to the floor between his front paws. Keep the treat close to his nose as you lower it as if the dogs nose and the treat were magnets.

As you get closer to the floor, your dog should lean down and eventually bend his elbows. When his elbows and belly touch the ground, mark, and turn your hand over to present the treat. If he is not going all the way down, reward him for small approximations of the final behavior (examples: head down, elbows slightly bent, getting closer to the floor). After you are able to get him all the way down, and reinforced with the treat in your luring hand three or four times, remove the treat from your hand and try again. If he follows your hand into a down, mark, and treat from your other hand.

Continue until your dog is doing it fairly proficiently, then add the cue "Down" one second before you use the hand prompt. After a few reps, your dog should start to preempt the prompt when he hears the down cue. At this point, you can fade out the hand prompt if you choose; however, if at any point he does not go down after the cue, use the hand prompt rather than repeating the cue. Try to avoid putting your hands on the dog to add pressure for him to go down.

To teach down from a stand, repeat the steps above, but with the dog in a standing position. It may take a bit longer, but hopefully he should go down fairly quickly. If not, try moving the treat from side to side once you have it near the ground. This sometimes creates added interest in the treat, and causes him to investigate closer, which can result in the down.

How to train "Drop it"
https://youtu.be/E-RgusQ_XBo

Start by playing tug with your dog. Once he's engaged, hold the toy very still, up close to his mouth, and say "drop it" one time, and wait. Don't talk to him, look at him, or try to pull the toy from him. In fact, try to avoid adding any tension of your own. Eventually, he will get bored and let go. Immediately say "take it," and give it back to him. Play tug for five to ten seconds, and repeat the "drop it" cue. He will start letting go quicker, so that he can continue playing. If he is struggling to let go, hold a treat to his nose. Say "drop it," and when he releases the toy, mark, and treat. Immediately present the toy again, and say "take it."

Make sure you don't get him too amped up during the tug sessions in the beginning, or it will be difficult to get him to drop it. Once he understands the game, you can gradually amp him up more. Practice with lots of different toys to help him generalize the behavior to anything he may have in his mouth.

How to train "Leave It"
https://youtu.be/2a6uYDsWcDs

When training with food, it is important to teach your dog to have impulse control. After all, you don't want him mugging your hand every time you have a treat in it, or taking food from you at any time, for that matter, without you offering it to him.

Here are three steps for teaching your dog to "leave it"

1. To begin, hold a treat in your closed hand, and present it to your dog directly under his nose. Let him lick and paw at your hand. Make sure you ignore all behaviors until he looks away, and instantly mark, and toss the treat behind him. After he retrieves the treat, repeat the game. At some point you will notice that he will just stay back when you present your hand, because the treat is going to come from behind him. Once he is reliably leaving the food alone, say "Leave it" just as you present the food. Make sure that you always mark the behavior of staying back from the food, so that it is clear when he is allowed to have the treat.

2. Repeat step one, but with an open hand. If he approaches your hand, close it. If he stays back, mark, treat, and repeat.

3. After you have successfully repeated steps one and two several times, place the treat on the floor. You may have to practice the open hand

several times closer and closer to the floor to help your dog succeed. Once you have placed it on the floor, your dog will most likely approach it. Say "leave it," and cover it with your hand. If he backs away, remove your hand. If he returns, just cover it up again. If he stays back, mark, and treat with a different treat. Leave the treat on the floor, and add another to the pile. If he stays back, mark, and treat with another treat. Continue this several times until you have a small pile of treats on the floor. When the game is over, pick up the food, say "take it," and let him have this big jackpot reward.

How to train "Come when called"
https://youtu.be/02JDafkaIBE

To many dog owners, this is the holy grail of dog behaviors. It's the inability to do this behavior that gets many dogs labeled as stubborn and strong-willed. Let me say as the pet parent of a rescued Dachshund, I completely get it. The thing is, it doesn't have to be that way.

Most puppies start off as velcro pets, constantly clinging to your leg no matter where you go, including the bathroom. This behavior is partially to blame in that it leads us to a false assumption that they will always be that way. So we don't bother to train a recall. Six months down the road, we are suddenly dealing with an independent-minded adolescent that seems to have forgotten that you exist, except at mealtime. Sounds a lot like our human teenagers. The best way to avoid this is to teach a rock solid recall right from the start. One that is in the dog's mind, very beneficial for him to respond to. But not to worry, if you've already hit, or passed, that adolescent age, the following techniques can work for you as well. This is not to say that it will not be challenging, and the more they have practiced ignoring you, the more difficult it may be.

Step one: Teach them their name. If you have not actively done this, please refer to the "Training your dog's name" section. After you have taught them to look at you by calling their name, in a low distraction environment, preferably indoors, hold a treat in front of them, and say *"Rover* (insert your dog's name) Come," and back away. When your dog catches up to you, touch his collar, mark, and treat very enthusiastically with lots of praise. Also, remember to keep the cue very upbeat and positive. When he is doing this well starting directly in front of you, try again with the dog a few feet away, making sure to back away as you give the cue. The motion will help attract your dog. When he reaches you, touch his collar, mark, and treat. After a few reps, practice with the treat out of sight, and when the dog reaches you, touch his collar, mark, and treat. Only do this for a few reps per session, and then randomly try it throughout the day.

Step two: Play hide and seek. Start by popping out of sight, just around a corner. Call your dog, and when he shows up, touch his collar, and throw a big party with lots of treats and praise! Randomly do this throughout the day. After some practice, begin making it harder to find you.

Step three: Take it outside. Use a long leash, so that you can control the distance your dog can move away from you, and repeat step one. As your dog gets better up close, increase the distance he is allowed to move away from you.

Step four: With the use of an assistant, take turns calling the dog away from the other. Call your dog, and when he reaches you, touch his collar, mark, and treat enthusiastically. Have your assistant call the dog from you.
As he calls the dog, stand up straight and ignore the dog, as to make it easier for him to leave you and go to where he is called. The assistant should reward and praise as you did when the dog reaches him. Then the cycle repeats.

Come when called should be practiced every day, always with enthusiastic praise and treats.

A few tips:

1. Never call your dog to punish him. If you need to stop a behavior always go to him.

2. Don't only call your dog to end play, or to come inside. Spend time in the yard with your dog, and periodically call him to you. Reward him, and immediately release him to go play.

3. With the use of a long line, practice this at different locations.

4. If your "Come" cue has previously been poisoned, try using a different cue like "Here."

How to train "Place"
https://youtu.be/7q_SLaj-ZR4

One of the most useful behaviors you can teach your dog is to go lay on a mat. Although we all love having our dogs close to us, there are times when it's just not practical. Here are a few such instances where showing your dog how to relax on a mat can really be beneficial.

1. When guests come over.

2. When you are performing chores around the house like cooking, cleaning, and laundry.

3. When you have two dogs, and you want to train one without the distraction of the second dog.

4. When watching tv, or any other time you don't want your dog underfoot.

To teach place, hold his bed in your hand, and as your dog is watching, lay it in the middle of a room. As your dog approaches it to investigate, mark, and treat by placing the food on the mat. Say "Ok," and guide your dog away just a couple of feet, and wait. If he returns to investigate the bed further, mark, and treat. If he does not return to the mat, move the mat with your foot slightly to spark his interest. If he returns, mark, treat, and say "Ok" as you guide your dog away. Repeat these steps until he is intentionally returning to the mat every time. When he returns to the bed, begin to require more - like his front feet on the bed, all four feet on the bed, sitting on the bed, and laying down on the bed. Remember to always place the treat on the bed when you pay him. This will encourage him into a down, especially if you have previously taught the down position, and you hold your hand on the treat for a few seconds before letting him have it.

If you are struggling to get him to go to the bed, guide him to the bed with your hand pointing to the bed as you walk toward it. When his front feet touch the bed, mark, and treat, say "Ok," and guide him off. Repeat in the same manner as instructed above. Once he is going to the bed regularly, start from a little further distance away. Point to the bed, and if he goes to the bed, mark, treat, and say "Ok" as you call him off of the bed. If he does not go when you point, walk toward the bed as you point, mark, treat, and repeat.

Continue to add distance until you are able to cue him from anywhere. Take it slow. If at any distance your pup is failing, get closer to the bed before pointing, so that you don't build frustration into the behavior. After he is going to the bed every time, add the cue "Place" just prior to pointing. Practice several times, and he should start going to his bed from your verbal cue.

Why do we say "Ok"? Ok is what's referred to as a release word. If you prefer to use a different word, like "free," that's fine. The point is that you are signaling to the dog that it's ok to leave the bed. When teaching the place cue, you are not including any duration on the bed, but by adding the signal right from the start, your dog may start to understand that "Ok" means the behavior is over, and he is free to leave the bed. If you slowly add duration before saying "Ok," you are building in a default stay. Just make sure you don't add duration in the beginning. You want to make the going to a mat behavior as easy as possible.

How to teach "Stay"
https://youtu.be/lroO-SQ6zeM

Stay is one of the most important behaviors you can teach your dog, but teaching a reliable stay can be a challenge. As with other behaviors, it's important to teach this behavior in a way that is easy for the dog to succeed. If he's failing over and over again, it can be frustrating for the dog, and cause any progress you have to be slow at best.

Stay part one: Stay should be taught in two parts: duration and distance. So, for part one we will focus on duration up close with the dog in a down. Tip: If you have trained a dog to go to a bed, it will make this behavior much easier, because the edge of the bed creates a boundary that makes it a bit more clear for the dog - especially if the bed is raised slightly.

With your dog in a sit or down, feed him treats in rapid succession at first (teaching the stay from a down is

85

easiest). With some puppies, it's hard to get the food to them fast enough. As they start to realize the food is coming to them room service style, so it's not necessary to move, you can slow down your delivery, but be systematic about it. Once you can go 5 seconds between treats, try 10, then 15, and so on. Make sure you stay at each interval for several reps before adding more time, and if you find that your dog is failing a third of the time or more, you may want to remove a few seconds until he is being successful at least 80% of the time before adding time. This may seem slow and tedious, but I assure you it's much quicker than being successful at a short duration, and skipping to a long one, and it makes it much easier for the dog.

Tip: Lightly exercising your dog prior to working on "stay" can help.

Stay part two: Distance is a bit trickier. With your dog in a down, shift your weight back on your heels, and return immediately to your original position. if your dog has stayed in position, mark, and treat. After a few reps, try to take one step back, and immediately return to your original position, mark, and treat. Proceed by adding more and more steps, making sure to repeat each interval several times before adding steps. Do not add any duration when you step back. The idea is that you're attached to your dog like a rubber band being stretched, and you return swiftly after taking the step, or steps, back. Mark, and treat, on each return. Note: although you are not intentionally adding duration, the fact that it takes longer to return with every step you take is slowly adding duration, but at a pace that is much easier for your dog.

Proofing the stay: After you have been successful at both of the steps above, and have added considerable distance for several sessions, you can begin proofing the behavior by adding distractions, and small periods of time when you will go out of sight.

With your dog in a down stay, step back 3 to 5 steps, and begin stepping to the side one step, and then back to your original position. Mark, and treat. Then take two steps to the side, then three, and so on, until you can move all the way around your dog. When you are successful in one direction, move the other way around your dog.

When you have success with all the steps above, start adding distractions like walking funny, dancing, bouncing a ball, and dropping food. Amp up the distractions slowly, so your dog has the best chance at success.

If at any point your dog breaks the stay, just direct him back into position, and start again. If you are not using a bed, just get him back to the same place on the floor that he was before he broke.

Add the "Stay" cue

You may have noticed that in the directions above, I never asked the dog to stay. This is because until he understands how to stay, he will probably break often, causing you to repeat the cue often. This will make it difficult for your dog to understand, or possibly cause the cue to become meaningless. Instead, wait until it's obvious that your dog understands what he is supposed to do, then try again, but this time, after you ask him to sit, down, or go to his mat, say "Stay," and present your palm toward him as you step away. Repeat the steps above for a short duration, release and reward your dog, and try another rep.

The release cue

The most important part of teaching a stay is the release cue. This is a signal that lets your dog know that it's ok to get up or move out of position. Without it, there is no clear communication that lets the dog know that the stay is over, so your dog may choose to get up at any time. To teach the cue, say "Ok" when the stay is over, and encourage your dog to move. When you are first teaching the stay, you should free your dog frequently, so they can rehearse waiting for the release cue, and to make it easy for them to be successful at the stay. Say the release cue every time, and your dog will start to learn to wait for the cue.

Teaching stay at doorways

Does your dog bolt out the door when he wants to go outside, or do you struggle to keep him from pushing past you to get out of the car at the dog park? My favorite place to use the stay cue is at doorways or gates. A dog bolting through a doorway to get outside is a disaster waiting to happen.

Here's how it works. Approach the door with your dog. If the dog goes toward the door when you put your hand on the door knob or handle, immediately pull your hand away, and wait. If your dog backs away or sits, reach for the knob again. If he stays back, open the door. If at any point he moves forward, close the door quickly, and wait for him to back up or sit. Repeat this process until he stays back for a few seconds, and say your release cue "Ok." Then let him out. Practice this at all exterior doorways and gates. Add a bit of duration each time before giving the release cue. Once he understands that he is to wait, practice walking out the door without him, and then releasing him. Take it slow, adding one step toward the door at a time, and eventually all the way out before releasing him. If he tries to run out, block him with your body, and start the process over. It's a good idea in the beginning to keep him on leash even if going out to a fenced yard, so that you can stop him if he manages to push past you. Be consistent. Don't make your dog a gambler by only requiring this some of the time.

How to train
"Loose leash walking"
https://youtu.be/pAK5NlpHRlk

Walking your dog can be a pleasant experience, but for most, it can be challenging, and at times extremely frustrating. For starters, having your dog walk beside you can be a bit unnatural for him. If you step back and watch a dog, you'll notice that they don't tend to walk in a straight line, their pace is erratic and often much quicker than ours, and their nose is often to the ground. Dogs learn so much through their sense of smell. Their olfactory system is at the top of their sensory intake. It's how they determine if the environment is safe or unsafe, if there are other dogs around, if food is available, and other such things. When we put a leash on our dog, and take him outside, then expect him to walk by our side with no sniffing around, and to only be allowed to go where we lead them, it can be a tremendous source of stress. It would be much like if someone led you to a busy street, blindfolded, and asked you to hold their arm and follow.

By allowing our dogs to take a little time to check out the environment, and do what dogs do, it can alleviate much of their stress, and make it much easier for them to listen to instruction. Learning to communicate with them about what we want, without adding stress to the situation, and giving them some choices, will make it easier for the dog, and for us.

So how do we begin? When training a dog to perform any task, it should always be in a way that is easiest for him to understand, and with a high rate of reinforcement. So let's break it down.

Ten steps to an easier walk

1. Since dogs have a strong need to take in the environment, we should begin training loose leash walking in an environment that doesn't offer much in the way of stimulation. Showing a dog how to walk near you, and change direction when needed, is much easier when their focus is on you. So choosing a non-distracting training space, perhaps in your living room or other space that they are familiar with, is the first step. Only after they learn to focus on you, walk, and change direction without tension on the leash indoors, should you even consider going out.

2. Focus exercises are the first things you should work on. After all, if you cannot get your dog's attention,

communication is impossible. (See the section on teaching your dogs name and "look at me").

3. With your dog on a six-foot leash, stand in front of your dog, facing him, and begin to walk backward, turning every few feet in an erratic, unpredictable pattern. As you take your first step, say "let's go." As your dog starts to walk, continue to talk to him with lots of praise and excitement. If he gives you eye contact, mark, and treat at a very high rate of reinforcement.

4. Make sure that each time you turn, you repeat a cue like, "let's go," and when he catches up to you, mark, and treat. Don't forget to engage with him. Talk to him a lot and make him love being near you.

5. After making several turns walking backward and facing your dog, turn, and encourage your dog to walk by your side doing the same zig-zag pattern. If he goes past you, and goes

to the end of the leash, give a cue like "slow," and STOP immediately. Make sure you don't pull on the leash, but keep it near you so that the stop is obvious. If he remains at the end of a tight leash, wait. When he backs off, say "let's go," and continue walking. Repeat this each time he gets to the end of the leash. Note: you may only get one step in before stopping in the beginning. Just be patient, and relax. Remember, he is just learning the rules.

6. After he has had lots of practice indoors, and seems to be "getting it," take it outside. Be sure to start in a place that is familiar, like your backyard. Make it simple, and as easy as possible, by starting with some free time to go sniff and take in the environment before walking. If you are not in a fenced yard, I would suggest using a long lead (15 ft.) to give him space for this, and just cinch it up to approximately 6 feet when you are ready to practice walking.

7. After he has acclimated to his surroundings, begin doing lots of focus exercises, saying his name, or look at me, and reinforcing eye contact. Remember to use a high rate of reinforcement.

8. Begin walking backward just as you did indoors, and work your way up to walking next to him, repeating the same zigzag patterns as before.

9. Take lots of breaks to go sniff. In fact, this is one of the best reinforcers for loose leash walking that you can give him. After walking for a couple of minutes, say "go sniff," and drop the leash, or if your in an unfenced area, you can use a longer leash, and just gather it up when you are walking to about 6 feet. (Don't use a retractable leash. With a retractable leash, there is always tension on the leash, and that is what we are trying to avoid.)

10. Take it on the road. After several successful walks in the backyard, take it to the front yard, then the street

in front of your house, then around the block, then to the park, and so on. The goal is to add distractions in slowly. If you immediately take him to the park, you have gone too fast, and will more than likely encounter difficulties. Practice your "leave it" cue, placing treats along your path before hand, and asking your dog to leave it as you continue to walk. Mark, and treat, each successful leave it (See how to teach "leave it.")

With each new environment, you should begin at the same starting point. Don't expect that your dog is going to do great in the front yard because he was great in the backyard. This is especially true when going to the park or a pet supply store.

If you have a dog that is over reactive toward people, other dogs, or chases cars, it is not the same as dealing with typical distractions. This should be dealt with as a completely different behavior and should be done with the help of a certified professional trainer.

CHAPTER 8

Troubleshooting and Reducing "Bad" Behavior

The myth of the perfect Dog

Many of us dream of the perfect dog. One that would never do any of the so-called problem behaviors that normal dogs do. We think of a perfectly behaved dog that is asleep on his bed until summoned, obeys every command without hesitation, and never embarrasses us in public. The so-called 100% reliable dog that you hear so much about in dog training ads. In reality, every dog is unique, and some dogs, no matter how well they are trained, will ever fit the mold you have for them. Are you 100% reliable? In other words, is every decision you make a good one? Doubtful. If we can't trust ourselves to always make right decisions, how can we expect a dog to? It's important to be realistic with our training goals, and to train the dog you have, not the one you wish you had. After all, we can't all be rock stars, or theoretical physicists, and not all dogs are meant to be top performers in agility or obedience. Don't get me wrong, it is possible to change any behavior to some degree, but you need to realize that it can sometimes be very difficult, and may require more time than you are able to give. My suggestion to those who want a "perfect dog" is to buy one of those cool little robot dogs they sell in the big box stores. You won't even have to feed it.

Stop That!

Nearly every call I get is someone asking me how to stop their dog from doing

_____.

Whether it be chewing up their shoes, play biting, excessive barking, or pulling on the leash. They never stop to consider why their dog is doing what he does. All behaviors have a purpose, and the key to stopping behaviors we don't like is to try to figure out what that purpose is, and then show them a new way to access it in a way that is more acceptable to us.

So training works best when you focus on what you want your dog to do rather than what not to do. Here's an example: Your dog jumps up on you. Why? Most likely it's because he's happy to see you and wants to say hi. If your dog is a 180 lb mastiff that could be a problem. So what's the solution? How about showing him another behavior that gets your attention? Something like sitting, or pressing their side against you. Remember, dogs do what works for them. If sitting gets your attention, then sitting is what they will offer. Jumping up, on the other hand, gets them nothing. When you teach your dog the basic cues like sit, down, look at me, and others, it's part of a bigger plan. You are showing them what works. You are also giving them a voice. Helping them to communicate by expanding their "behavioral vocabulary." Just remember that if sitting, or some other relaxed form of communication, stops working, your dog will try other behaviors until he finds one that works, and it may not be one you like.

I suspect that a good portion of the people reading this book are having some issue with their dog and are trying to find a way to fix it. Many of you will be tempted to skip right to this section or perhaps directly to the specific topic you are needing help with. I urge you not to do this. Unless you have previous training experience, and a good understanding of behavioral science, you will be lacking crucial tools that make the following protocols work.

Most of the time when a family gets a new dog, they spend most of their time reacting to the dogs behavior rather than showing the dog what he needs to know to get along in a human controlled household.

Below is a list of common behavioral problems, and how they are usually handled in a typical household.

1. Dog jumps up on family and guests = Family pushes the dog off, yells at the dog to stop jumping, punishes the dog

by kneeing him in the chest, or hitting him, and sticking him outside.

2. Dog soils the house when the family is away = Family returns and yells at the dog, rubs his nose in it, and puts him outside.

3. Dog chews up the owners shoes = Dog gets yelled at, hit, or put outside.

4. Dog digs through the trash while owner is away = Owner yells at the dog, shames him on facebook, punishes the dog by hitting him, and placing him outside.

5. Dog barks and lunges at the fence as strangers walk by = Owner yells for the dog to shut up, buys an anti-bark citronella collar that sprays the dog in the face when he barks.

6. Dog drags his owner down the street when on leash = Owner jerks on the leash, kicks him in the ribs, buys a choke, prong, or shock collar to control the dog.

7. Dog does not come when called =
    Owner chases after the dog, punishes
    him, keeps him tied up outside,
    or buys an electric shock collar or
    electric fence.

8. New dog doesn't get along with
    the other dogs = New dog gets put
    outside, re-homed, or taken to the
    shelter.

9. Dog play bites his owner = Owner
    sprays him in the face with a water
    bottle or holds his tongue down.

10. Dog ignores commands given by his
    owner = Owner yells at the dog or
    inflicts harsh punishment.

In every one of these cases, better
communication (training), management,
and leadership could have made all the
difference. Waiting until the dog offers a
behavior that you are not ok with, or just
gambling that they never do, is just asking
for trouble, and is not fair to the dog.
Not to mention, it's incredibly stressful
for you. So what are we to do? In the

following pages I will explore six of the most common behavioral problems, and show you some techniques that have been proven to work in most cases. But before doing so, let's look at something that can have a significant effect on most behaviors, preserve your sanity, and give your dog a better quality of life: How to relax.

Take a chill pill

In my opinion, the greatest thing you can teach your dog is how to relax. When I first got my GSD, I immediately had images in my head of this crazy, over the top, out of control dog. So to curtail this, I thought I had to exercise him as often and as hard as possible. Unfortunately, I realized after doing this for a while that I was creating the very dog I had imagined. It seemed that the more I exercised him, the more energy he had. It seemed hopeless until one day I had an aha moment while reading an article online about exercise building stamina.

Of course! I was creating an athlete with no marathons to run. I'm not saying you shouldn't exercise your dog, but there is a balance. I was so focused on wearing him out that I never even considered showing him how to relax. Mornings kept getting earlier and earlier, and I even hung a flood light in my backyard, so I could exercise him late at night.

Fortunately for me, and him, I came to the realization that things had to change, and I began studying about relaxation techniques for dogs. I gradually reduced the amount of exercise he was doing (a work still in progress), and began implementing the relaxation protocols. Although he has a ways to go, it was the best decision I ever made for him. Now I teach it to all of my clients, and I have found it to be a tremendous game changer. If you have read the sections of this book teaching downs, lying on a mat, and stay, you will already have some of the necessary tools to do it properly.

Ten, Nine, Eight, Sev...zzzzzzzzz

Yoga Dog

1. To begin, make sure your dog has burned off some energy through mental stimulation, or through light exercise.

2. Place a mat next to your chair, and call your dog to the mat. (See "place" cue)

3. Begin rewarding every second or two. Make sure you don't mark before

treating, and place the treat on the mat near his head quietly and calmly.

4. Slow down the treat delivery over time. Don't do this too quickly. If he starts breaking the stay, treat more frequently.

5. Don't talk to him, and don't make eye contact.

6. Over time, he will begin looking away or lowering his head. He may also yawn, begin blinking more often, shifting to more comfortable positions, or stretching. Reinforce all of these behaviors every time at first, and slowly look for calmer and calmer behaviors.

7. Practice this in lots of different places around the house, in the yard, and eventually the park and other public places. Make them low-distraction environments at first, and then gradually raise the distraction level.

8. Reward your dog periodically throughout the day when he is doing absolutely nothing. Remember, behaviors that are reinforced grow in frequency. This includes laying around chilling out.

9. Use that amazing nose. Place several scents around the yard, such as lavender or jasmine, and let your dog sniff around. You can purchase Adaptil which is a calming Pheromone from your veterinarian. Spray it on his mat or on a bandana to place around his neck.

10. Give him a Kong full of treats, and place him on his matt.

Tip: Teaching a rock solid stay is helpful before doing these protocols.

Jumping Up

Imagine if you were two feet tall and greeted everyone you love at the knees. That's the world our dogs live in. Dogs have been bred for centuries to enjoy the company of humans. Jumping up to get our attention is sometimes the only thing the dog can think of to fulfill this overwhelming desire to be closer to us, and to be a part of our world. To be fair, we don't make it easy for them. We usually send them mixed signals right from the start. Allowing, or even encouraging, them to jump up to get attention with a resounding "Hi buddy, what a good boy!" I mean, who doesn't enjoy a cute little ball of fur jumping up to greet us. It seems that every fiber of their being is reaching out saying "I love you, please pick me up, and love on me." So of course, we accommodate. At this moment, we have just shown the dog how to get attention. Then later, when we are busy, and can't accommodate the pup, we scold them, and push them away when they greet us in this fashion. It's confusing to the pup, but at the same time makes the jumping up behavior even stronger.

Consider this: The last time you put your money in a soda machine, and it took your money, did you push the button once and walk away when nothing came out?

Highly doubtful. More likely you pushed that button over and over. When that button didn't work, you push another and another. Possibly trying even the flavors you don't like. Eventually, you give up. At least until the next time you want a soda, then odds are you will probably try again. Especially if there are no other machines, and that has been where you always get your soda. Only after it stops working consistently will you decide to give up completely, and bring a soda from home. At that point, you may possibly have a bit of animosity toward the machine. You may even have a few choice words toward it when you walk by. When something has worked in the past, then suddenly stops working, it can be incredibly frustrating. We will usually try our best to make it work again. At some point, we may give up on it all together, but usually not before it becomes a source of irritation.

So what does this have to do with dogs? If jumping up has worked to get your attention, jumping will continue. If your strategy to make them stop is to punish them, then you are still offering them attention, and with most dogs, some attention is better than no attention. Even if it's negative. If your strategy is to ignore them if they jump, this could work; however, just like in the soda machine example, if it suddenly stops working, they can get frustrated and try even harder, or offer other unwanted behavior like nipping or pulling at your clothes. For this reason, It is important to show our pups ways to get our attention that is acceptable to us.

Teaching them to sit on approach, or another behavior, is a great way to do this. (See How to teach sit) Once your dog knows how to sit, ask them to sit, take a few steps back, and lure them to you. Raise your hands up toward your chest and wait. Don't ask him to sit. The motion of your hands will probably prompt him to sit. If he sits, reinforce with treats, pets, and praise, and then quickly back up. If he sits on approach, reinforce. If he does not, back up again, and try holding your hands up toward your chest. Reinforce the sit. If at any point he jumps up on you, turn your back to him. Wait a few seconds, and repeat the exercise. By doing this exercise, you are showing him what works, and what doesn't work, to gain access to the consequence he was looking for. If you practice it a lot, this will become the dominant behavior for getting attention when he comes to greet you. Just make sure you don't ignore this new behavior, or it will fade, and you will end up back a square one or worse, a really frustrated dog that will jump even more.

But what about jumping on guests? Obviously, you can't ask your house guests to run through these exercises. Ideally, your dog should never have the opportunity to jump up on people. This brings us back to management.

If the cable man, for instance, comes to the door, your dog should be in a kennel, or another room, until they have learned to have four on the floor around guests. If friends or family come to visit, you should have your dog on a leash, and restrain them from jumping on your guests. Keep your dog at a distance for several minutes until the excitement of your new guest has worn off. Then ask your guest to pet your dog. If he remains calm, try letting him off leash. If he tries to jump up, hold him back, and wait a bit longer. As with everything you teach your dog, it's about being clear and consistent. If he becomes over-excited, or out of control, it would probably be best to put him in another room, and practice first with someone less interesting. Just make sure you give him something to do to help him relax. An over-excited dog can become destructive if he is focused on what is going on in the other room. A Kong stuffed with treats, or a bully stick, can be a great help with this.

It's best not to ask your dog to sit before letting your guest pet him. You want your dog to feel like he can leave at any moment. Always pay attention to your dogs reaction to your guest. If he acts unsure about meeting them, don't make him.

Chewing

This is a subject that is brought up a lot with puppy clients of mine, and for good reason. All puppies will chew at some point. In fact, it's a necessary part of their development. Not really what you wanted to hear right? Puppies need to chew. It relieves the pain of teething, and it is one way that puppies explore the world around them. Think about it. Even human babies are constantly putting things in their mouths. Our job is to make sure those objects are safe and appropriate.

But my puppy chewed up my expensive shoes! Ok, and where were your shoes when this happened? Oh, they were lying in the floor next to your puppies bed. Leaving objects like socks, shoes, clothing, and food wrappers out where your puppy can get them, and then scolding them for what only comes naturally to them, is not training. It's reacting, and this is something we want to avoid. Especially if we are frustrated. Once again it comes back to management. If you don't want your shoes chewed up, keep them out of the floor.

I used to have to tell my teenage son this all the time. It's amazing how many adults still have not learned this. Just as with potty training, if you are not able to directly supervise your puppy, they should be confined to an area that is puppy-proofed such as an exercise pen, crate, or a room with dog appropriate toys available only.

If your puppy is being supervised, and starts chewing on something that is not a dog toy or a dog chew, take whatever they are chewing on away, and redirect

their chewing activity to something that is allowed. I understand
that this may sound simplistic, and you're right. First, you have to be able to get the object from your dog before he has destroyed it, which can sometimes prove to be difficult. Second, your dog has to like the chew toys you
are offering in exchange.

Let's take the first challenge. Teaching a puppy to "drop it" is fairly simple to teach. (See training Drop it) The trick is, once they understand the cue to drop it, practice it a lot at times when it is not necessary. Make it a game. Play tug with rules such as: they drop it when asked, and leave it when asked. Just make sure tug is never instigated by your puppy, otherwise, he will be looking for things to grab in hopes of getting you to play with him. For this reason, all interactive toys, such as tug ropes or stuffed animals, should be put away when you're not playing with your puppy. This gives you leverage. You are in control of when the game starts and ends, and this keeps those toys interesting and exciting.

This brings us to the second challenge: making sure your dog is into the toy you're redirecting him too. Most dogs love playing with toys, but often we buy toys that we think look fun, and then find that when we present them to our dogs, they could care less about them. There are several reasons your dog may seem uninterested in toys. Usually, it's because we drop them and walk away, leaving them with a lifeless piece of rubber or rope lying on the floor that they may investigate and play with if we are lucky, but probably not for long, or more than likely they will just yawn and walk away from it. Remember, dogs are prey animals, and they love to chase. They also have been bred to be social.

This means they love interacting with people. So you're an integral piece of the puzzle. Make that toy come alive! If it has a squeaker, make it squeak. Pretend you have the best toy in the world. Play with it, and act like you want to keep it for yourself. Show it to him, and run away. Move it around like it's a little animal. Drop it, and then grab it again. If your dog goes after it, play tug with him. Make sure you let him win. Remember, you are trying to build interest in the toy. If you always win, he may decide it's no fun.

If your dog is not used to this kind of interaction, this may take some practice. Another option is to use toys that you can stuff with treats or peanut butter. If it's a hard plastic toy like a Nylabone, or other hard chew toy, you may have to ruff it up a bit with sandpaper, and rub peanut butter or cream cheese into the grooves. The more time you invest in the toy, the more they will be interested in it. Then when you need it for redirection, you will have serious leverage.

There are some toys that should be left out all the time. Kongs, teething toys like Nylabones, or other hard rubber toys, can be left out for your pup to chew on. Just remember, you may need to help them find interest in them at first. Once they start chewing on them, they will probably continue anytime the need to chew arises. This means they are not chewing on your pillows.

The goal is to build a habit of chewing on appropriate things, and if other competing things that are not appropriate are equally available, building that habit can be difficult.

Play biting

As an owner of a GSD, I feel your pain. Literally. When my dog, Loki, was young, he earned the common nickname, Land Shark. He loved to play, and that usually involved him using his mouth. First, it's important to know that this is a perfectly normal behavior. I often get calls from clients worried that there is something wrong with their puppy. Stating that their three-month-old puppy is aggressively biting.

While very rare, this could be a serious disorder, but in the vast number of cases, it's just a puppy being a puppy. If you watch puppies with their littermates, you will see that this is the primary way they interact with one another, and it's a good thing they do. In fact, many times adult dogs that are very mouthy, and have a hard bite in play, do so because they were removed from their litters too early. Those early days when they are with their mother and littermates are crucial in so many ways. Learning to have good bite inhibition, otherwise known as a soft mouth or soft bite, is near the top of the list. It would be nice if there was a magic pill that would keep a dog from ever biting, but since there isn't one, it's far better to teach a dog to have a soft bite than to not bite at all. At least while they are young. Once they have learned to have a soft bite, it's not difficult to eventually teach them that teeth to the skin is unacceptable, and doing it in that order may just save you a trip to the ER some day.

All dogs have the potential to bite. Even that sweet Golden Retriever that seems to love everybody. Every dog and every human for that matter has a tipping point, a trigger that can set them off. If they have never been shown how to control their bite, the reaction to that trigger may have serious consequences. In human terms, it's like someone that skips the argument and goes straight to fighting.

To teach a soft bite, play with your pup using a tug toy. Don't encourage your pup to bite your hand. They will most likely offer that behavior all on their own. When it happens, allow soft bites, but if they get harder, say OUCH, act like it really hurt, and walk away with the toy, ending the play. Make sure that you don't jerk your hand away. This may encourage him to go after it. You want to make the "ouch" obvious enough that he temporarily lets go, then gently remove your hand. Be consistent. All interaction with your puppy has to come to an end, and toys put away, every time there is a hard bite. Wait a couple of minutes, and resume play. If you notice your puppy's biting becoming more gentle, repeat this process but require lighter and lighter bites. You want him to think that humans are incredibly fragile. Eventually, end the play anytime their teeth touch skin at all.

All interaction between the puppy and young children should be supervised, and anytime the puppies teeth touch your child's skin, you should remove the puppy immediately. Children must be taught how to calmly interact with their new puppy.

Here are 10 rules all young children should follow when interacting with a puppy.

1. Only play with the puppy when adults are present.

2. Don't pat the puppy on top of the head or pet him roughly.

3. Never pick the puppy up without assistance from an adult.

4. Never tease the puppy, or play tug with him, unless the puppy has learned to play gentle and with rules such as drop it and leave it.

5. Don't take food from the puppy.

6. Don't hit the puppy.

7. Never feed the puppy treats unless supervised by an adult.

8. Never pin the puppy down.

9. Never drag the puppy by the leash.

10. Never put their face in the puppies face.

If you are having trouble with an adult dog who bites, it is a bit more serious. Usually, even the most mouthy puppies eventually grow out of it unless they are encouraged to bite; but for those who adopt an adult dog, and discover that he is mouthy, any teeth on the skin should not be tolerated, even in play. It is very difficult to teach an adult dog bite inhibition. For this situation, all play or interaction should end anytime they touch your skin with their teeth, even if it's an accident. For instance, if you are playing tug, and his teeth graze your hand, say "too bad," and put the toy away. For more severe cases, where your dog is acting aggressively, you should hire a certified professional dog trainer, or behavior consultant. Children should never have access to an adult dog who bites.

Barking

Barking can be one of the most frustrating things to deal with. Especially if you have close neighbors, or if you live in an apartment. It's also one of the ways our dogs communicate. So, when considering a course of action to reduce this behavior, we need to be cautious. First, we need to consider what the cause of the barking is. What's the purpose behind it? Dogs bark for many reasons. To scare off an intruder, to alleviate boredom, to tell another dog, or person, to back off because they are nervous, to get attention, or as a way of asking for or demanding something. I think we can all agree that barking is a good thing if there is an intruder in your home. Equally as important is the warning bark to tell an approaching dog or person to stay away if your dog is unsure about them. We often scold our dogs for such an outburst, but If you consider the alternative, a bite with no warning, a bark, although sometimes embarrassing, is much better.

So, it's not wise to try to stop all barking which is why using bark collars, shock collars, or removing your dog's vocal cords should not be an option. But what about those other times when barking seems to be more like a "spoiled child" throwing a fit because you didn't buy them a candy bar? Or when they seem to bark for no reason at all?

Let's tackle that last one first. All behavior has a purpose.

Just because we don't see it does not mean it's not there. Most of the time when a dog seems to bark endlessly, it's because they are bored. Solving this is sometimes as simple as playing with your dog, and making sure they have adequate exercise and mental stimulation. Dogs are social animals which means they need interaction with people or other dogs. If they are left out in the yard all the time, they will usually find some way to alleviate boredom and loneliness. Barking often fulfills this need. If your dog is driving the neighborhood crazy with its constant barking, it's simple: bring him indoors. Dogs should not have to live outside. Yes, they are animals, and their ancestors lived outside, but humans chose to bring dogs into our lives, and in doing so we have selectively bred them to need social interaction with humans. They are not the same as wild animals.

You may be thinking, what if they are constantly barking indoors even after their needs are met?

First, rule out any medical issues. I would advise consulting with your veterinarian. Undiagnosed pain or anxiety disorders can be the the cause of a host of behavioral problems.

I want to play, and I want it now! This is something I experienced with my own dog. Despite lots of attention, affection, and play, if my dog Loki decided he wanted me to go outside and play with him, he would start barking. So to "shut him up," I accommodated him. Basically, he was training me through negative reinforcement, and it worked. Barking got me out of my chair. Unfortunately, it also taught him that barking worked, so the barking behavior grew. Positive Reinforcement.

Yes I know, I'm a dog trainer, I should have known better, but sometimes it's not about what you know, but rather what's easy at the time. Believe it or not, there are many medical professionals that still smoke. Finally, I got my head screwed on straight, and decided to do something about it.

To begin, I considered what the consequence was in this situation. He got attention and play. Then, what was he doing to get that? Barking. Now whats the golden rule of training? "Consequence drives behavior." Playing, and giving him attention, was reinforcing the barking.

Solution

1. Stop reinforcing the barking by ignoring him, and even separating him from me if he barks, by putting him in another room for a few minutes. If he continued to bark when he was let out, I would just separate him again.

2. Figure out another behavior he could do to let me know he wanted to play frisbee. One that was acceptable to me. Loki already knows how to go to a mat, or lay down, and stay. So if I thought he might be getting ready to start barking, I would ask him for a down stay. Wait for about 5 minutes. Give him his release cue, and walk to the door. I would not say "let's go play," or anything that I thought would get him overly excited. I just quietly walked out with him, and pulled out the frisbee, and the game was on. Best of all, it happened without a single bark. After several reps, I started noticing

that when he got restless, he would walk over near where I was sitting and lay down. I would wait a minute or so then say "ok," and go outside with him. He had figured out a new way to communicate that he wanted my attention and the great outdoors. This is so much more pleasant than barking.

Of course I can't go out with him every time he comes and lays by my side, but by doing this consistently for a week or so, and "negatively punishing" him if he barked, by separating him from me for a few minutes, the barking was drastically reduced, and for a German Shepherd, that's a pretty daunting task. If your dog does not already know a down stay, see the section on ("Stay"), or try another behavior like having them give you their paw, or sitting. I like the "down stay," because it's the opposite of high-energy play. It shows him that relaxed behavior leads to fun things.

Stop Barking on cue
Another way you can reduce barking
is to teach your dog a cue like "Quiet."
The easiest way to do this is to find a
trigger such as the doorbell, or someone
knocking on the door, that makes them
bark. Have a friend, or family member,
knock at the front door. As soon as your
dog barks, say "Quiet" just one time, and
hold a treat in front of his nose. When
he stops barking to investigate, wait a
couple of seconds, mark, and treat. *An
alternative if you don't have an assistant*

is to record the doorbell, and play it for your dog. Repeat this at random times throughout the day.

If you are having an issue with your dog barking because of reactivity or aggression towards people or dogs, I would recommend contacting a local science-based trainer or behavior Consultant.

Digging

Dogs love to dig. Most would do so if left alone for long. My dachshund is a master excavator, especially when the moles are active. She loves it so much, and luckily for her I don't mind, but other pups may not be so lucky. So the first step in solving this puzzle is to ask yourself why. Let's look at the common reasons dogs dig, and explore some possible solutions for each.

1. To alleviate boredom - Often dogs are left outside for hours at a time. If they are not given something to occupy their time, they will look for something to entertain themselves, and what could be more fun than digging a big hole. My first suggestion would be to bring them inside unless you are in the yard with them. I understand that this is not always possible, so if this is the case, here are a few other ideas that can help. A. Exercise your dog. A tired dog is a happy, less destructive dog. B. Give them more attention. C. Leave a frozen food filled Kong, or two, and some other chew toys, to help keep them occupied.

D. Fill a plastic swimming pool with dirt, and hide treats and toys under the surface. Encourage them to dig in the swimming pool by showing it to them and digging up one of their toys, showing it to them, and burying it again in front of them. Make it a game. Keep a close eye on them while they are in the yard, and if they start to dig anywhere else interrupt them and redirect them to the digging area.

2.   Hunting moles or other subterranean critters - Moles eat grubs. Spread insecticide for removing grubs, and your moles should leave. You may need to keep them out of the yard for a day or so until it has had a chance to absorb into the ground.

3.   To escape or gain access - Supervise your dog while they are outdoors. If you see them trying to dig under the fence, interrupt them, and call them to you. When they come away from the fence, play a game of tug, fetch, or chase. The idea is to

show them that staying in the yard is reinforcing. Never leave a dog outdoors unsupervised if they are an escape artist unless it is in a enclosed pen with a top and a concrete bottom, and make sure your dog always has updated tags on their collar if they are outdoors.

4. To get cool in the summer heat - Summertime can be tough on dogs that are left outdoors. Make sure they have plenty of water and shade. Make sure to limit their outdoor time with lots of breaks to relax indoors.

5. To bury a bone or other item - For whatever reason, dogs sometimes like to bury their bones, and other chew toys. The best solution I've found for this is the same as in 1.A a designated digging area.

Stealing food from the trash

Our modern canine companions are descendants of feral dogs who, to survive, lived around garbage dumps and scavenged for food. Our pups no longer need to do this, but that behavior has been passed down through their DNA. In short, it's normal dog behavior, but one that can be incredibly annoying to us.

So how do we change this? Well, as I've stated before, it starts with management. Trash cans should be kept in a cabinet, or closet, that latches, so the dog never has the opportunity to repeat the behavior. If this is not an option, use a trash can that has a lid with a latch. These suggestions are a little inconvenient, but not nearly as much as constantly picking up trash. Spray trash cans with citrus spray, or other deterrent sprays, to discourage them from getting in it. You should also teach your dog the "leave it" cue, just in case they do try to get in the trash, and you catch them in the act.

A Word About Corrections

You may have noticed that up to this point I have not I mentioned correcting your dog. So do I use corrections? What is a correction? A "correction" is the buzzword dog trainers use as a nice way to say punishment. I have been accused of being a "positive only" trainer. The premise of the accusation is that I let dogs get away with anything, which is just not the case. It is true that I don't use physical corrections in training, such as a pop on a prong collar, or a smack on the nose with a news paper. Mostly because there is no need. Dogs are capable of learning without being aversive, and physical corrections (positive punishment) can have unwanted consequences such as causing your dog to become aggressive, or causing them to shut down and become unwilling to train. Do I ever use a physical correction? Sure, in the case of an emergency where my dog may be injured. Examples would be that I might have to jerk on his leash to pull him out of the way of an oncoming car for instance, or push him away from something he is trying to eat that may do him harm. The fact is that life is not "positive only." There are plenty of things that your dog might find aversive without us adding to this. In my opinion, our job is to teach our dogs in a way that does not add to their stress, but instead helps them to cope with the aversives that already exist in their environment. Using a combination of training, management, and good communication, you can teach your dog to be a well-behaved dog without ever raising a hand to them.

Conclusion

Dogs are an amazing species! They are funny, loving, brilliant, and fun to be around. They are also quite often a necessary part of our lives. It is amazing how the fate of our two species have become so intertwined. When you consider the origins of dogs, and their rich history, it's easy to see that they not only enjoy being with people, they need us. Unfortunately, humans sometimes have a bad track record of letting them down. If you don't believe me, go visit your local dog rescue. They are over run with dogs who have been given up on, or in some cases, abused. I mentioned in the introduction of this book that I love dogs. It is my hope that by writing this, maybe we can, in some small way, remedy this problem. The first step in helping any relationship, whether it be human relationships or interspecies, is communication. When it comes to our dogs, training, management, and building a bond by spending quality time with them, is how we communicate. Hopefully this book will give you an idea of how to do this.

Resources

Below are some excellent training resources that I recommend.

Paws Companion Dog Training YouTube Channel
(The videos for this book and others)
https://www.youtube.com/channel/UC8E19Ar-M-xKNjjNcZlGUuA

My Facebook page
Facebook.com/pawscompaniondogtraining

Grisha Stewart
http://grishastewart.com/

Kikopup YouTube channel
https://www.youtube.com/user/kikopup

Simpatico dog training YouTube channel (one of my favorites)
https://www.youtube.com/channel/UCMgKNPC0O91FgvS94YMglag

Zak George YouTube channel
https://www.youtube.com/user/zakgeorge21

Association of Professional Dog Trainers
https://apdt.com/

International Association of Animal Behavior
Consultants
https://m.iaabc.org/

The Pet Professionals Guild
https://www.petprofessionalguild.com/

Dog Star Daily
https://www.dogstardaily.com/

Reading recommendations

Don't Shoot the Dog by Karen Pryor
Culture Clash by Jean Donaldson
Chill Out Fido by Nan Kene
The Power of Positive Dog Training by Pat Miller

Made in the USA
Columbia, SC
25 July 2020